THE GARDENER'S D.I.Y.

by

Michael Roberts

Edited by

Sara Roadnight

Photographs and Illustrations by

Michael Roberts

To my mother
Patricia Roberts

Published by Gold Cockerel Books

ISBN 0947870 22 9

Printed by Ashley House Printing Company, Exeter.
Telephone: (01392) 202320

Conditions of Sale

INTRODUCTION

This book came into being because, as an amateur carpenter, I would often see items in garden centres and catalogues, and would always feel I could make them myself for less money. Even the simplest wooden products these days seem to be outlandishly expensive, they always seem to come in a garish orange colour, and are not even made of treated timber.

I have constructed and used all the projects in this book myself, but I realise that they will probably be subject to various alterations and modifications by my readers as the local situation or individual whim dictates. I have tried to incorporate ease of manufacture into pleasing designs, although this has sometimes been adjusted by Sara when some aspect of the project has offended her artistic eye!

I have not said anything in the instructions about the time it will take to make the various items, because it will all depend on how quick you are, how mechanised you are and how familiar you are with making things in wood. You will note that I haven't used any special joints. Those of you who are carpenters and wish to include carpentry joints, can do so and make a better, stronger job of it.

I have used tanalised or treated wood in the production of all the items in this book. In the case of plyboard, I normally use best Canadian shuttering plyboard which has one good side and one rough, but you can use exterior grade ply if you wish, although it is more expensive. It is important to let tanalised wood dry out properly, and a word of warning, beware of splinters as the tanalising process makes them as bad as blackthorn and you could end up with a nasty septic wound.

I like to buy my timber from country timber yards. These are often attached to large country estates and you can find them in the Yellow Pages; their wood is far cheaper than what you would buy from a builder's merchant or superstore, and you can pick and choose exactly what you want.

I hope you will enjoy making these items as much as I have.

Michael Roberts & Sara Roadnight,
Kennerleigh, Devon **June 2000**

CONTENTS

CLOCHE

I wanted a cloche which was simple to make and store, and could be used, not only to keep the plants warm, but to provide shade with green netting, or protection from the birds for plants such as strawberries, so the basic design can be made with various different covers. Each cloche is slightly longer than the previous one so that they will stack, and they can be made in any length up to 6'. The ends can be blocked off with a slate or off-cut of wood.

These can be really quick to make, but do ensure that the angles of the lath on the plyboard are correct to obtain maximum strength. It is a good idea to paint or weatherproof the plyboard, particularly the ends.

Make a plyboard template first. Once it is made, then it is easy to make the others. Cut the small battens first A&B, but check the angles with the template. Screw the plyboard to the battens from the outside, and drill holes for the long lateral pieces, (48 ins.) Nail these on with 3ins nails, two per joint. If you want to make these cloches stack, just make them 1" shorter each time.

CLOCHE

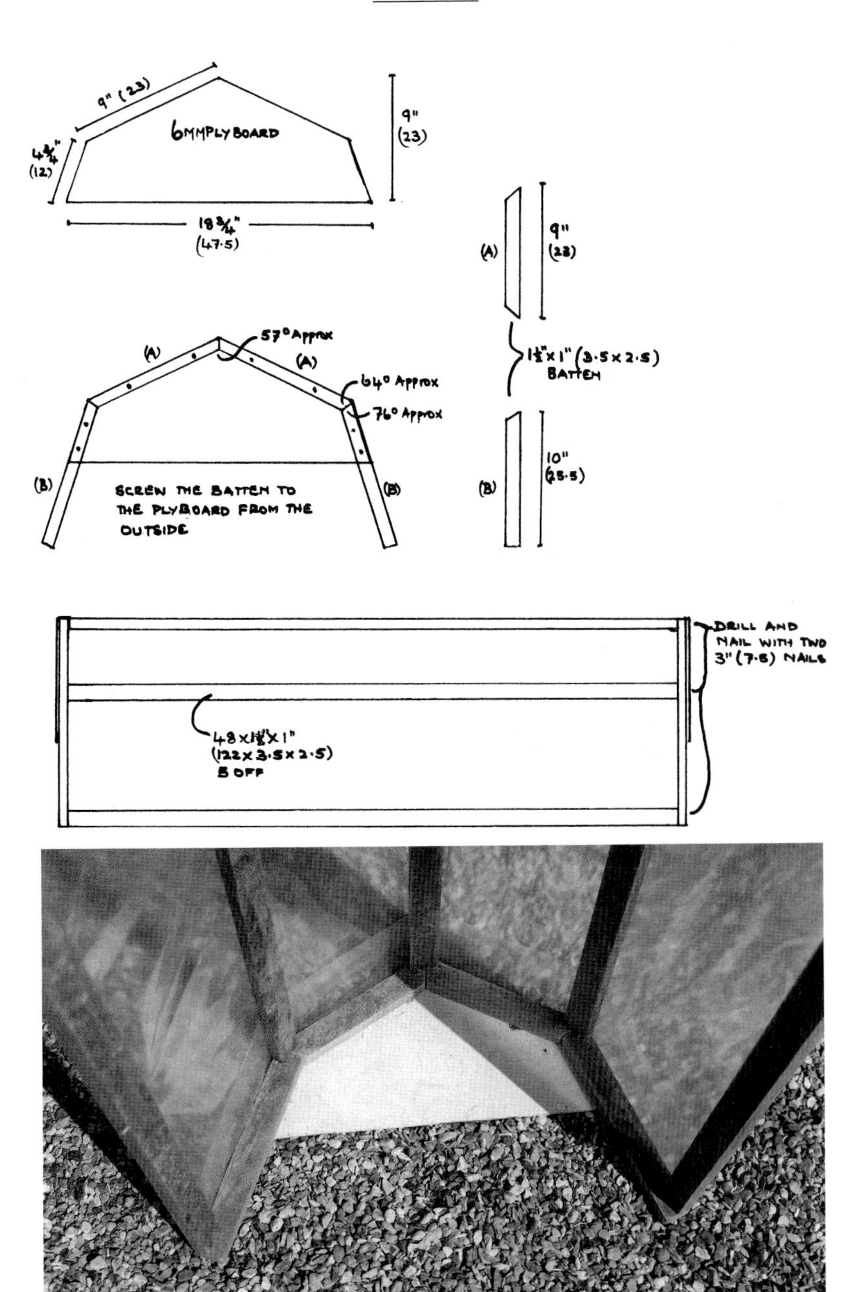

9" (23)
6MM PLYBOARD
4¾" (12)
9" (23)
18¾" (47.5)
(A)
9" (23)
57° Approx
(A)
(A)
64° Approx
76° Approx
1⅜"x1" (3.5 x 2.5) BATTEN
(B)
(B)
SCREW THE BATTEN TO THE PLYBOARD FROM THE OUTSIDE
(B)
10" (25.5)
DRILL AND NAIL WITH TWO 3" (7.5) NAILS
48 x 1⅜" x 1" (122 x 3.5 x 2.5) 5 OFF

LEAF GRAB

This leaf gatherer was inspired by two sayings, the first from Warwickshire which says ' The older you get, the further away the floor becomes,' and the second from Suffolk which says 'Do you get old, do you get artful!'

I wanted a long handled leaf gatherer especially for the senior citizen, that really works and picks up everthing, leaving nothing behind. This tool does the trick.

LEAF GRAB

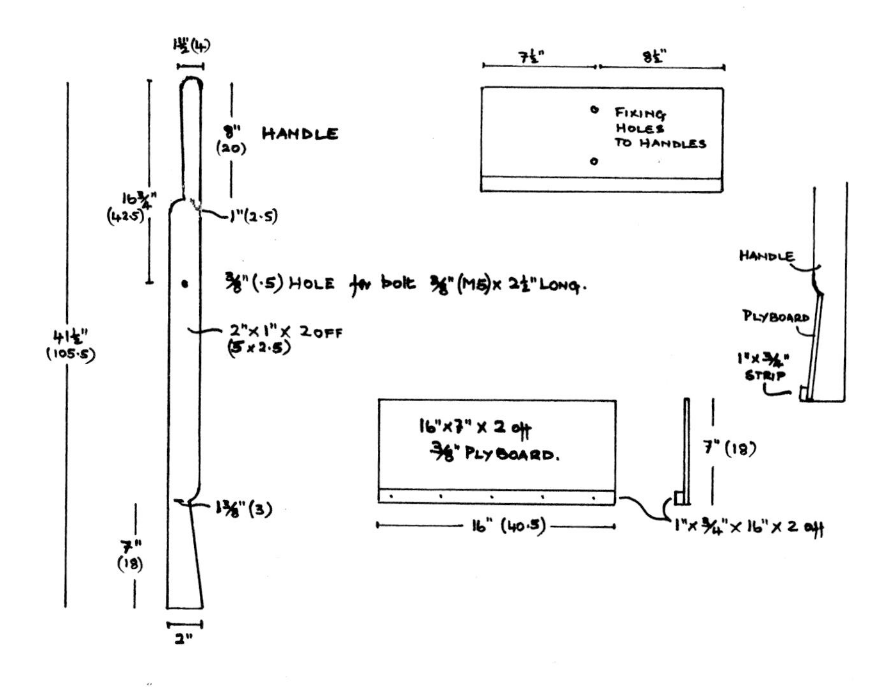

THE BOLT WILL NEED TO BE CUT TO SIZE, AND USE A SELF LOCKING NUT.

TOMATO BOX

Most people want to grow their own tomatoes as the ones you buy in the supermarkets are often quite tasteless. Using growbags, these boxes will ensure that your tomatoes are supported and off the ground during production; they also dismantle and stack for winter storage.

Years ago, our gardener used to have outside the greenhouse, a large rainwater tank, inside which was a hessian sack filled with sheep daggings, (wool which has sheep muck attached to it, clipped from around the tail area). It was like a giant tea-bag, and every now and then it would be prodded to turn the water in the tank a deeper brown colour! The tomatoes in the greenhouse loved this concoction and tasted wonderful.

Cut the timber to size and make up the base then add the feet. Cut the uprights to size and mark and bore the holes for the bamboo canes. Draw the upright supports, (4" x1") with the aid of a paint tin, cut out with a jigsaw and screw onto the uprights. Offer up this assembly and drill through the bottom to the base. Use a 3/8" x 2.5" galvanised gutter bolt to hold it in place. Mark each upright so next year you know which one goes where.

TOMATO BOX

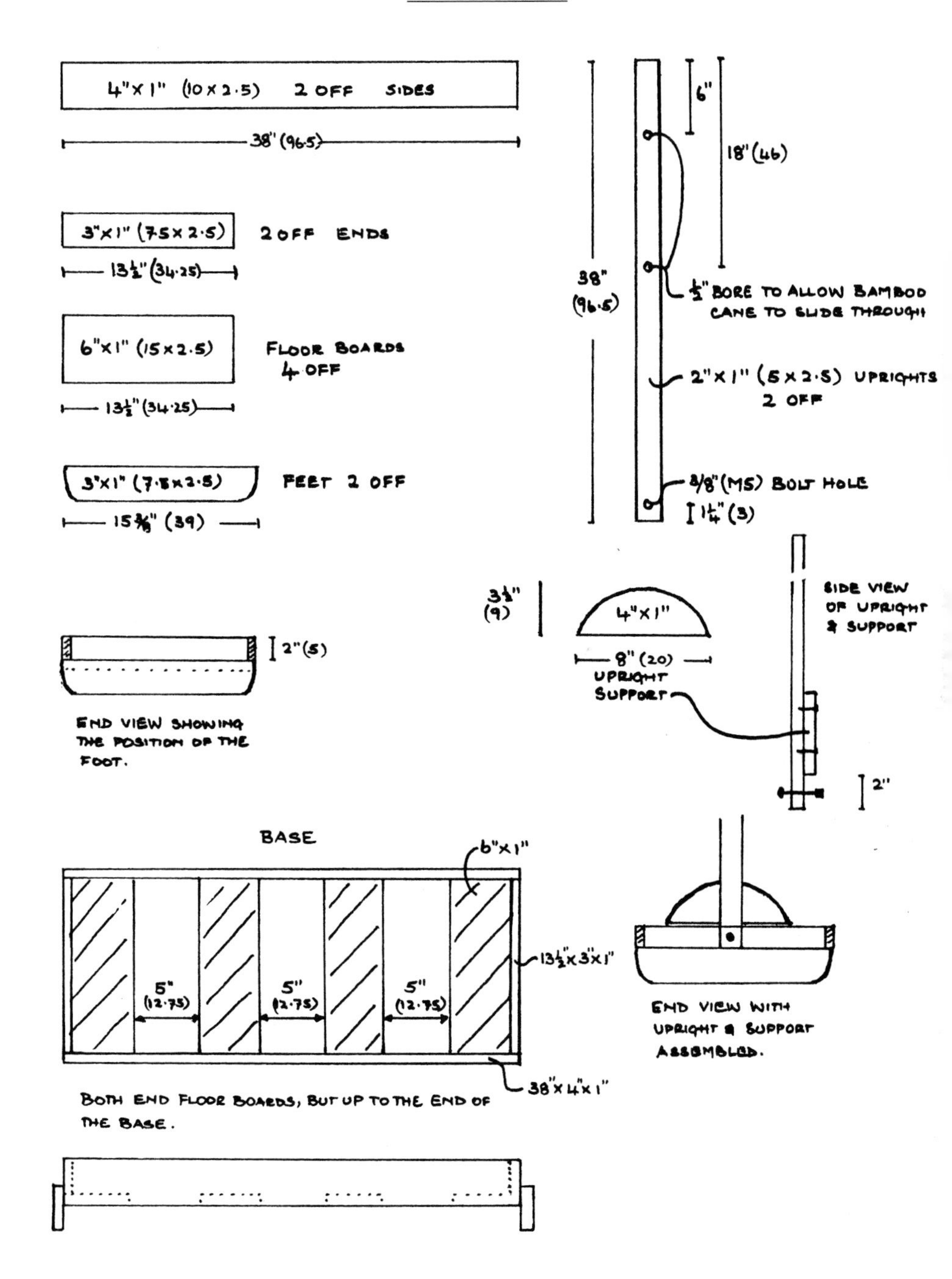

4"x1" (10x2.5) 2 OFF SIDES
38" (96.5)
3"x1" (7.5x2.5) 2 OFF ENDS
13½" (34.25)
6"x1" (15x2.5) FLOOR BOARDS 4 OFF
13½" (34.25)
3"x1" (7.5x2.5) FEET 2 OFF
15⅜" (39)
2" (5)
END VIEW SHOWING THE POSITION OF THE FOOT.
6"
18" (46)
38" (96.5)
½" BORE TO ALLOW BAMBOO CANE TO SLIDE THROUGH
2"x1" (5x2.5) UPRIGHTS 2 OFF
⅜" (M5) BOLT HOLE
1¼" (3)
3½" (9)
4"x1"
8" (20)
UPRIGHT SUPPORT
SIDE VIEW OF UPRIGHT & SUPPORT
2"
BASE
6"x1"
13½"x3"x1"
5" (12.75)
5" (12.75)
5" (12.75)
38"x4"x1"
BOTH END FLOOR BOARDS, BUT UP TO THE END OF THE BASE.
END VIEW WITH UPRIGHT & SUPPORT ASSEMBLED.

COLD FRAME

This a standard construction for a cold frame, but I have used a 4'x2' sheet of perspex instead of glass. I have done this for safety reasons, remembering only too well the time when, as a very young boy, I stood on a cold frame reaching greedily for blackberries and fell through! The scar remains on my leg to this day.

There are two sets of props either side to allow adjustment for the plants to harden off.

Remember, this type of cold frame will not withstand severe frosts, minus 5 or more, so a covering of an old blanket or sleeping bag will be required. For the more experienced carpenter, halving joints can be incorporated into the roof of the cold frame.

Cut and make up the front and back panels, then fix on the sides. Cut the 2"x 2" for the roof and then cut out the perspex groove with a bench saw. Cut the centre bar in two at the same depth (1.25"). If you are not half jointing the corners, then drill and screw them together. I have added two galvanised corner plates to strengthen the top corners. Slide the perspex (4' x 2') into the grooves and then fix the top of the centre bar (23" x 2" x 5/8"). Drill and screw then add in the handle and four roof supports.

COLD FRAME

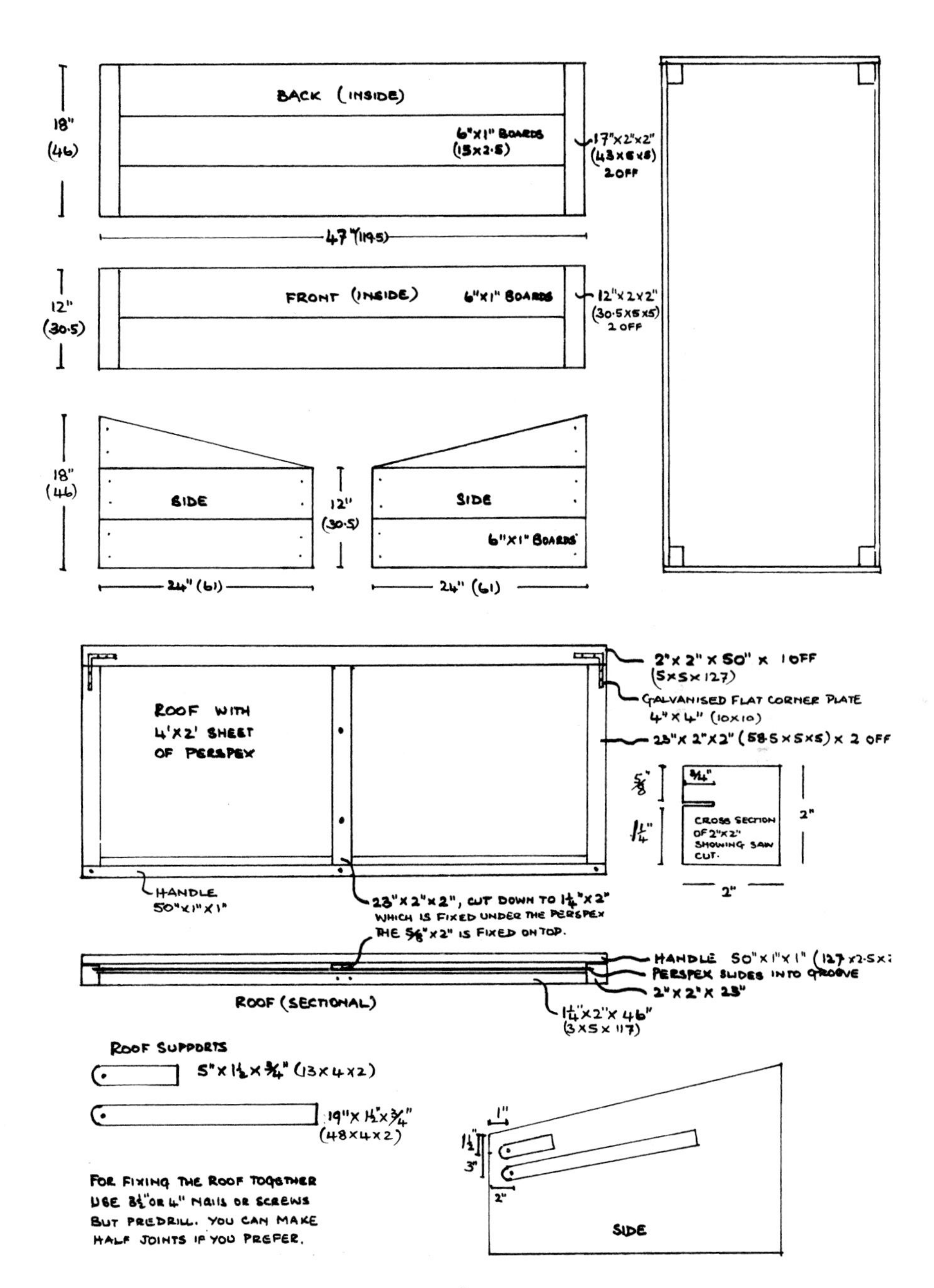

18"
(46)
BACK (INSIDE)
6"X1" BOARDS
(15X2·5)
17"X2"X2"
(43X5X5)
2 OFF
47" (119.5)
12"
(30·5)
FRONT (INSIDE)
6"X1" BOARDS
12"X2X2"
(30·5X5X5)
2 OFF
18"
(46)
SIDE
12"
(30·5)
SIDE
6"X1" BOARDS
24" (61)
24" (61)
2"X2"X50" X 1 OFF
(5X5X127)
GALVANISED FLAT CORNER PLATE
4"X4" (10X10)
23"X2"X2" (58·5X5X5) X 2 OFF
ROOF WITH
4'X2' SHEET
OF PERSPEX
5/8"
3/4"
1 1/4"
CROSS SECTION
OF 2"X2"
SHOWING SAW
CUT.
2"
2"
HANDLE
50"X1"X1"
23"X2"X2", CUT DOWN TO 1 1/4"X2"
WHICH IS FIXED UNDER THE PERSPEX
THE 5/8"X2" IS FIXED ON TOP.
HANDLE 50"X1"X1" (127X2·5X
PERSPEX SLIDES INTO GROOVE
2"X2"X23"
ROOF (SECTIONAL)
1 1/4"X2"X46"
(3X5X117)
ROOF SUPPORTS
5"X1 1/2X3/4" (13X4X2)
19"X1 1/2"X3/4"
(48X4X2)
FOR FIXING THE ROOF TOGETHER
USE 3 1/2" OR 4" NAILS OR SCREWS
BUT PREDRILL. YOU CAN MAKE
HALF JOINTS IF YOU PREFER.
1"
1 1/2"
3"
2"
SIDE

BIRD TABLE

Most people go out and buy a bird table without thinking about the design. The most common faults with "bought in" bird tables are first that the food becomes sodden because the roof does not overhang the table area sufficiently, and second that they are difficult to clean properly.

It irritates me when I sometimes see a nestbox incorporated into the roof of one of these bird tables, as no bird would be likely to use one in that situation. Mind you, if the weather is hard, the birds would not care about the design and would be grateful for any food, but if you are looking at this object every day through the kitchen window, it is nice to see something that pleases the eye.

There is a ceramic dish provided for water and a drop-down flap to allow for proper cleaning of the table area.

Cut and make up the base and cut out the water container hole, then cut and build up the sides. The holes in the sides are made with an interchangeable hole cutter which fits on the drill. Fix on the sides and side flap and then add on the roof pieces. The finials are made of plyboard, marked around a small paint tin and then drawn to a point. Give the roof two coats of Cuprinol and let it dry thoroughly.

Now cut out the floor support and rails. Dig or hammer in a post, depending on the soil, to a depth of 18", and ensure it is level on the top; if it is not then saw it level. Nail on the post platform with two 4" nails then slide on the bird table; with any luck it should be level.

The ceramic dish is an oven proof pie dish 4.75" or 5" wide.

BIRD TABLE

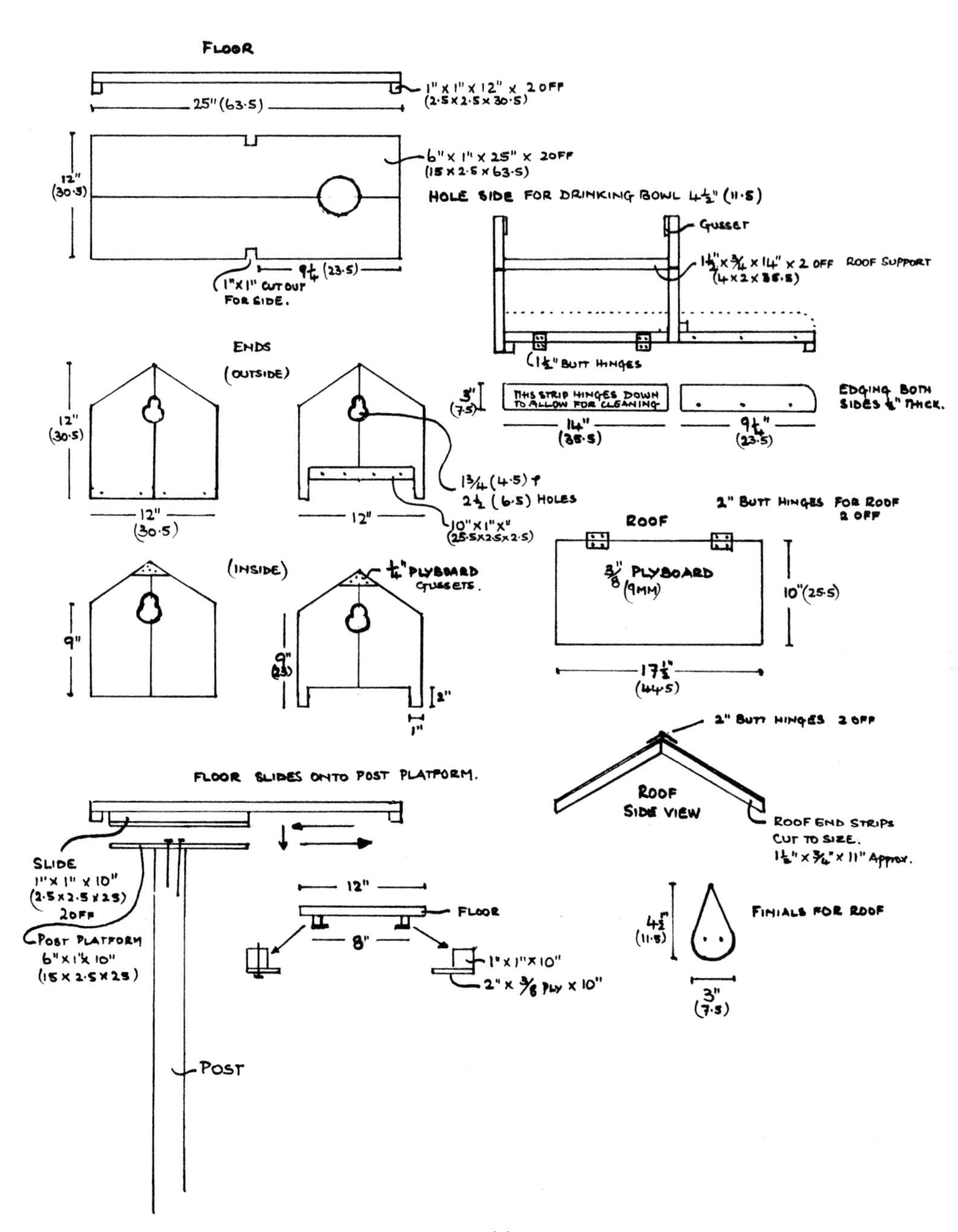

FLOOR
1" x 1" x 12" x 2 OFF
(2·5 x 2·5 x 30·5)
25" (63·5)
6" x 1" x 25" x 2 OFF
(15 x 2·5 x 63·5)
12"
(30·5)
HOLE SIDE FOR DRINKING BOWL 4½" (11·5)
9¼ (23·5)
1" x 1" CUT OUT
FOR SIDE.
GUSSET
1½" x ¾ x 14" x 2 OFF ROOF SUPPORT
(4 x 2 x 35·5)
1½" BUTT HINGES
ENDS
(OUTSIDE)
12"
(30·5)
3"
(7·5)
THIS STRIP HINGES DOWN TO ALLOW FOR CLEANING
EDGING BOTH SIDES ¼" THICK.
14"
(35·5)
9¼"
(23·5)
1¾ (4·5) &
2½ (6·5) HOLES
12"
(30·5)
12"
10" x 1" x 1"
(25·5 x 2·5 x 2·5)
2" BUTT HINGES FOR ROOF 2 OFF
ROOF
(INSIDE)
¼" PLYBOARD GUSSETS.
⅜" PLYBOARD
(9MM)
10" (25·5)
9"
9"
(23)
2"
1"
17½"
(44·5)
2" BUTT HINGES 2 OFF
FLOOR SLIDES ONTO POST PLATFORM.
ROOF
SIDE VIEW
ROOF END STRIPS
CUT TO SIZE.
1½" x ¾" x 11" Approx.
SLIDE
1" x 1" x 10"
(2·5 x 2·5 x 25)
2 OFF
12"
FLOOR
FINIALS FOR ROOF
4½"
(11·5)
8"
POST PLATFORM
6" x 1" x 10"
(15 x 2·5 x 25)
1" x 1" x 10"
2" x ⅜ PLY x 10"
3"
(7·5)
POST

GREEN HOUSE/SHED

When I designed this I wanted a greenhouse where I could bring on my vegetable seeds and also a shed where I could keep some of the tools and clutter one needs for gardening. I am pleased with this building as it gives me the best of both worlds and is really easy to make.

I have used a wooden floor, but there is nothing to stop you from putting the house on concrete or paving slabs. The ventilation comes from the hinged roof which can be raised; the roof also incorporates the gutter, and is chained so it cannot lift in a gale and blow away. I bought the half glazed door from the local salvage depot for £10.00.

There are two main points about the construction of this shed: first it must be built on a level floor otherwise the front glazing panel will not fit correctly, and second, it must face due south.

The inside layout of the shelves is not perfect, but I need to live with that for a season until I'm used to it. You may need to make adjustments, but the system works satisfactorily so far.

The plyboard must be painted with a wood preserver; use a good quality one like Sadolin which comes in a range of different colours. Paint the house first before fixing the perspex sheeting, and this must be secured with the correct type of fitting.

If you have always wanted a greenhouse but have limited space, I think you will find that this fits the bill very well.

Cut out and build up the floor. If you are going to use paving slabs or concrete, make sure that the site is level; you will need to nail some tanalised 3" x 2" onto the floor members of the four sections so that the plyboard is off the floor.

Cut the timber for the back; this is the largest section and you may need a hand to manoeuvre it into place. Cut the timber for the two sides and the bottom front panel.

The house/shed can now be bolted or screwed together.

Now fix in the top front rail and glazing bars. Cut the timber for the roof and nail on the fascia boards. Next add the perspex glass. It is very important to follow the fitting instructions exactly, and it is best to buy two pieces the right size and shape for the job. You will need a hand to get them into place safely, and once there, screw in the hinges and window opening fittings. I have also added a chain locking system, so on very windy days I know the roof will not blow away.

Next add the front perspex sheet. If the building isn't level the sheet will not fit, so you will spot that straight away. Fix it on carefully using the correct fittings. Attach the guttering for the roof and arrange the down pipe system.

Always ensure that the plywood has a chance to dry out and that there are no damp areas caused by leaks or items too close to the ply. If you paint it regularly with Cuprinol it should last 40 years or more.

Next it is time to organise the inside. I have designed a system which is different from that in the photograph as I was not entirely happy with that, but the new arrangement should work well. Happy potting in your new shed!

GREEN HOUSE / SHED

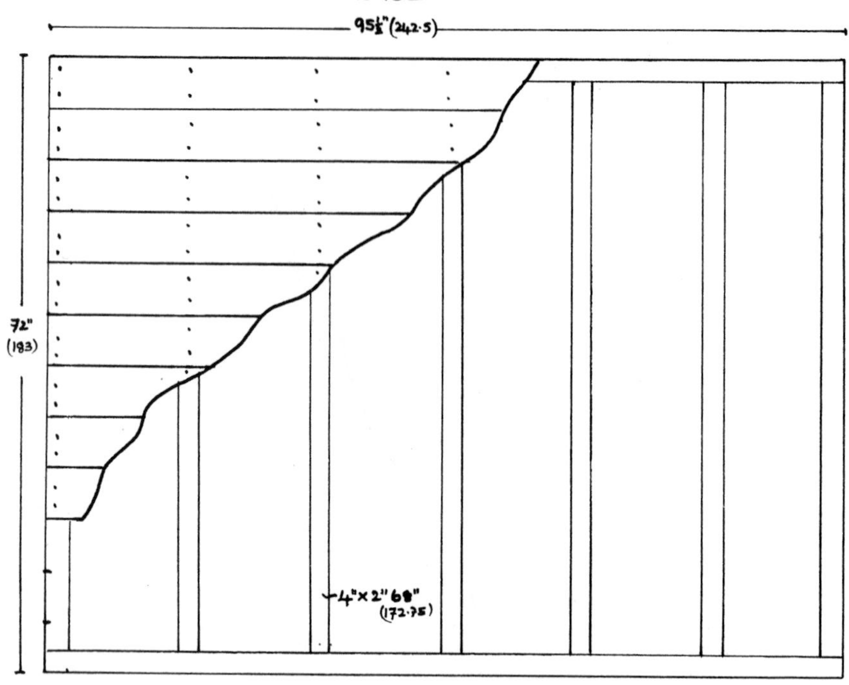

12 × 6"×1"×95½" FLOOR BOARDS
2 × 4"×2"×95½" HORIZONTALS
7 × 4"×2"×68" LATERALS.

6"×1" = 15×2·5CM
4"×2" = 5×5 CM.

FRONT

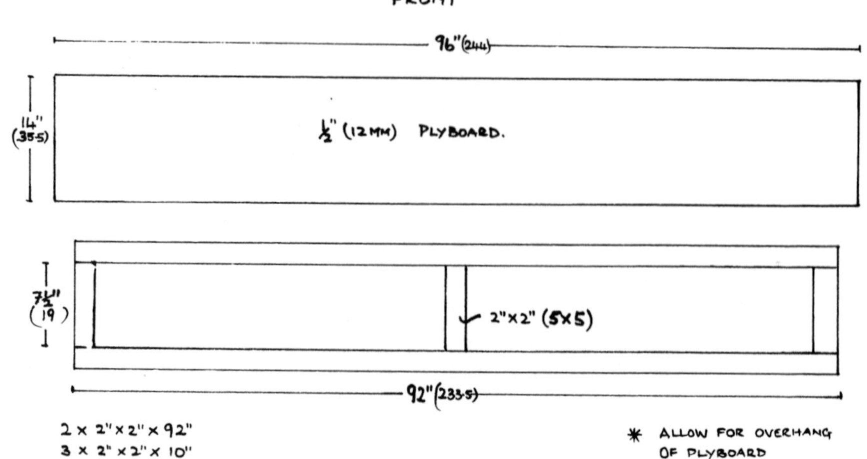

2 × 2"×2"×92"
3 × 2"×2"×10"

✱ ALLOW FOR OVERHANG OF PLYBOARD

GREEN HOUSE / SHED

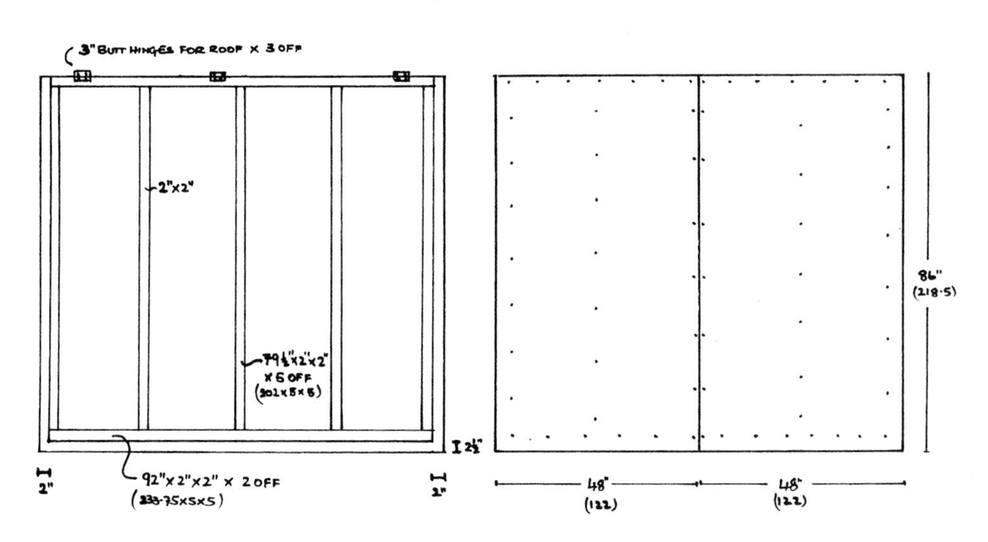

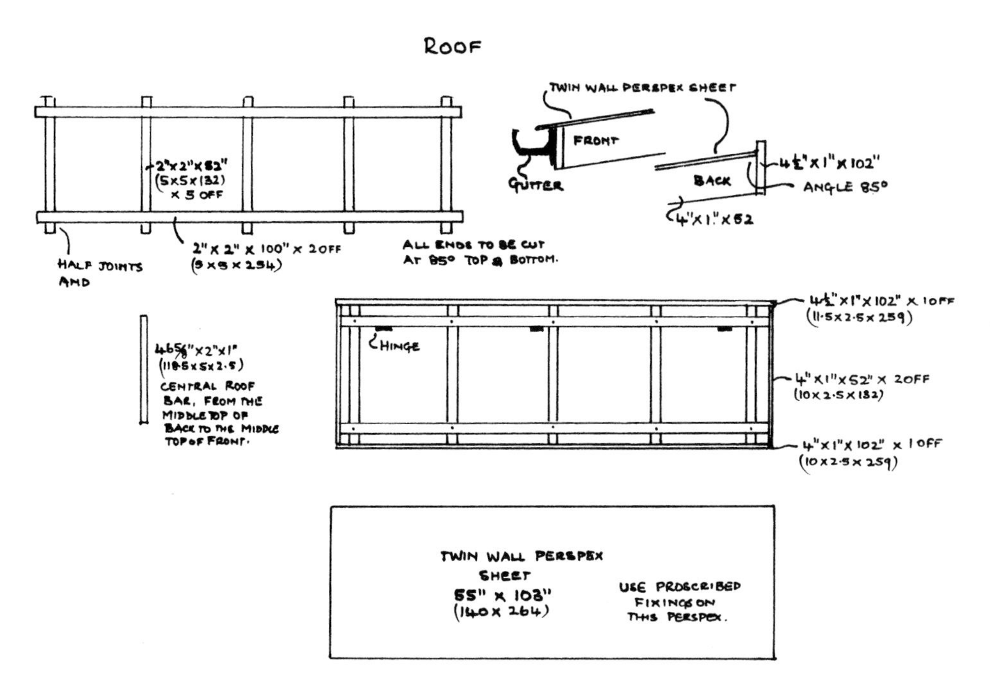

GREEN HOUSE / SHED

SIDES.

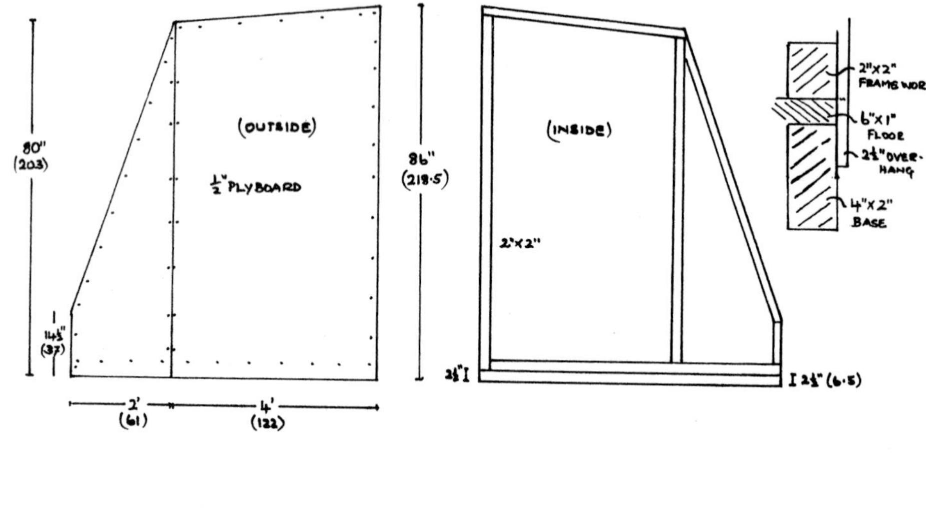

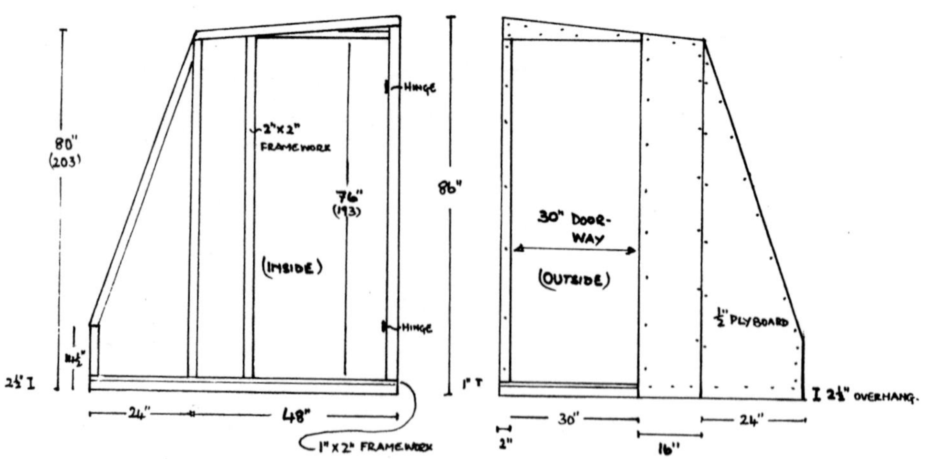

BUY A 6' 6" x 30" (198 x 76) DOOR FROM THE LOCAL SCRAP YARD, AND CUT IT DOWN BY 2". FAR CHEAPER THAN MAKING ONE.

GREEN HOUSE / SHED

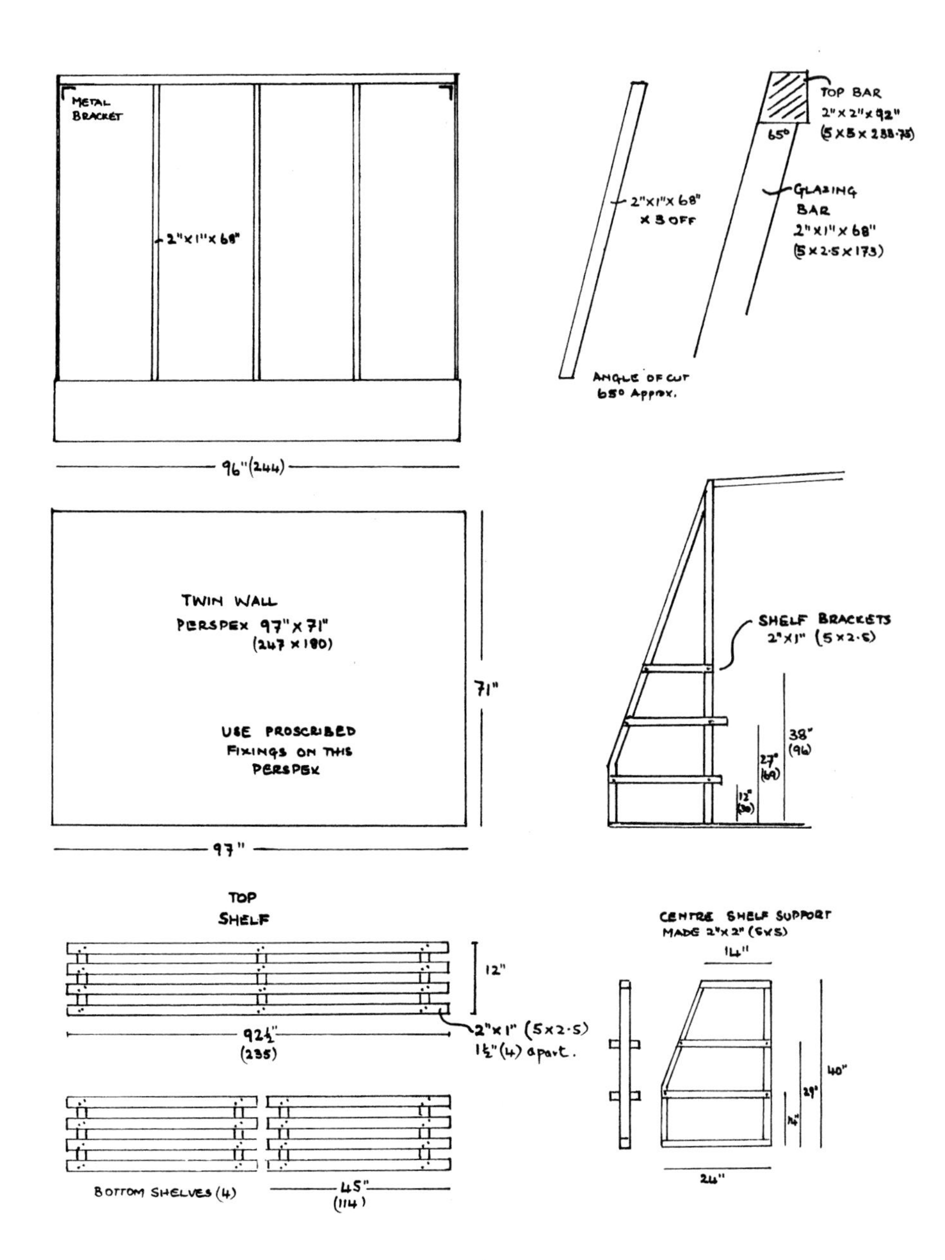

WALLCOTE

If you have ever thought about keeping a few doves in the garden but haven't got room for a dovecot on a pole, then this wallcote would be a good alternative.

I wanted a pigeon house that was practical, ie it was easy to clean and maintain, so I came up with the idea of making the house into a "chest of drawers" so that I could clean out one section without disturbing any of the other birds that might be sitting or brooding next door. It is easier to remove a nestbox, take it down and clean it on the ground, than climb 6 feet or so up a ladder and scrape the nestbox clean through a pophole!

Our doves here have taken to this wallcote very well and have reared several families so far. Location should be on an east or south east facing wall.

Make up the bottom oblong first then add the roof and the top shelf followed by the front top corner piece. Next cut out the back and back top corner piece and fix them onto the framework. Add the landing strips and 2.25" pieces under the shelves. The main house is now finished.

Cut the timber for the various nest boxes and fix them together. Make sure that they are a loose fit so that when you have painted the wallcote and it is thoroughly dry the nest box/drawers will slide in and out easily.

You will need a good strong rawlplug to fix the wallcote to the wall, and I have added a couple of picture brackets on the sides just for safety and peace of mind.

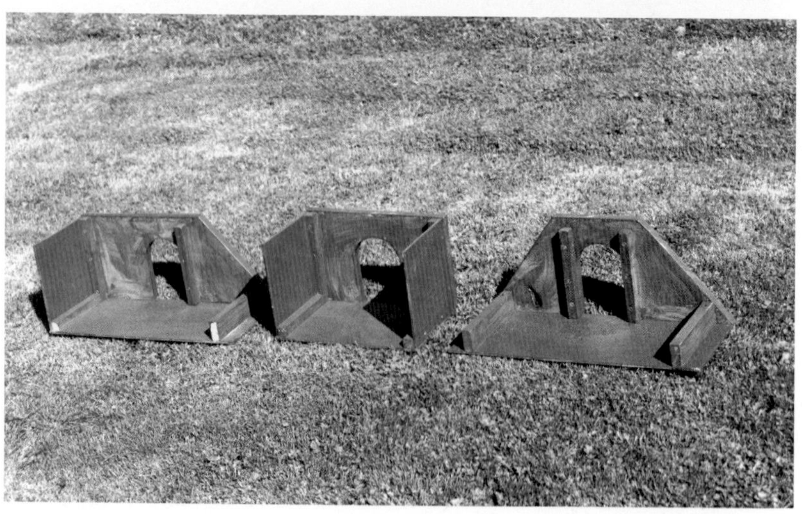

WALLCOTE (TIMBER THICKNESS 3/4" OR 2CM)

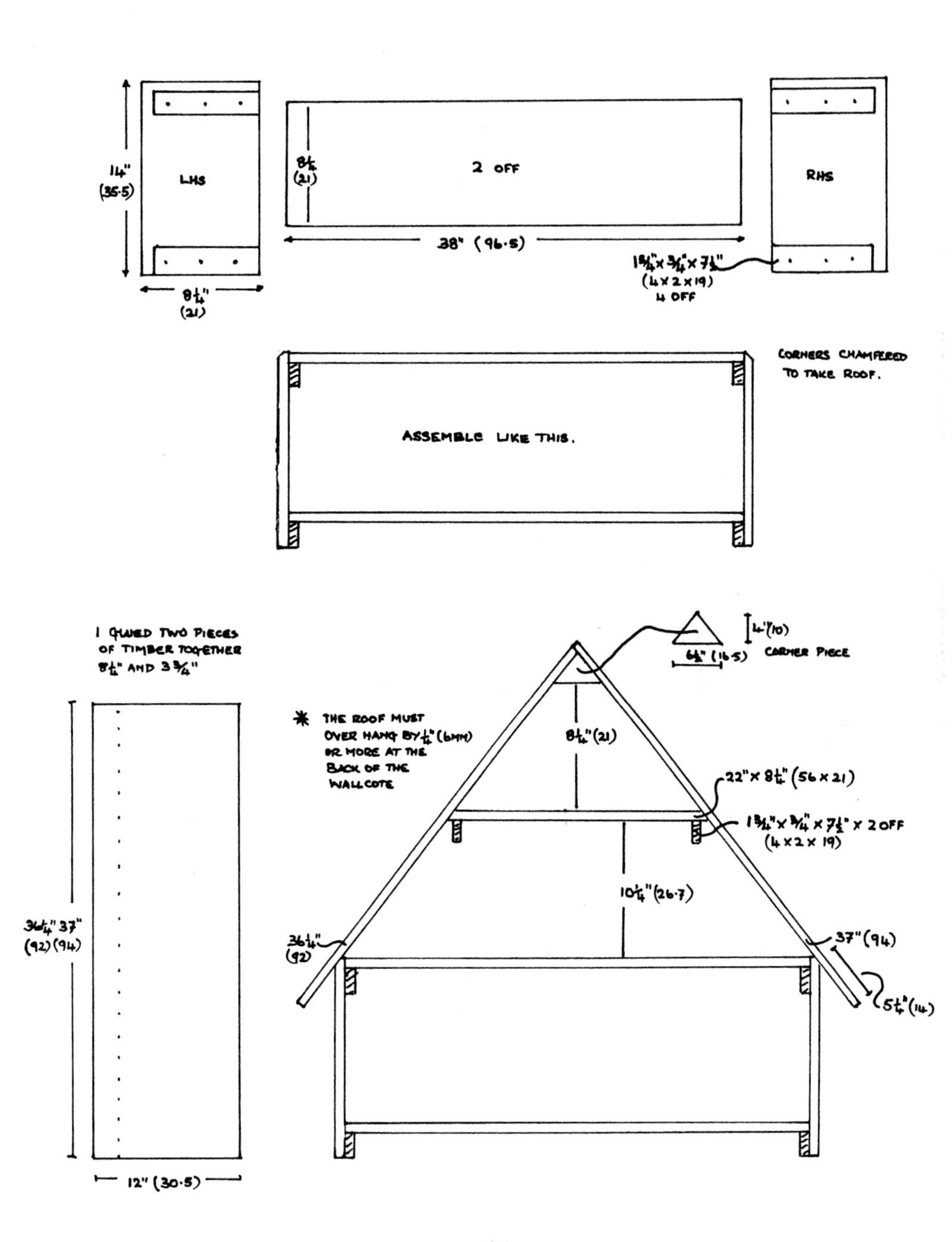

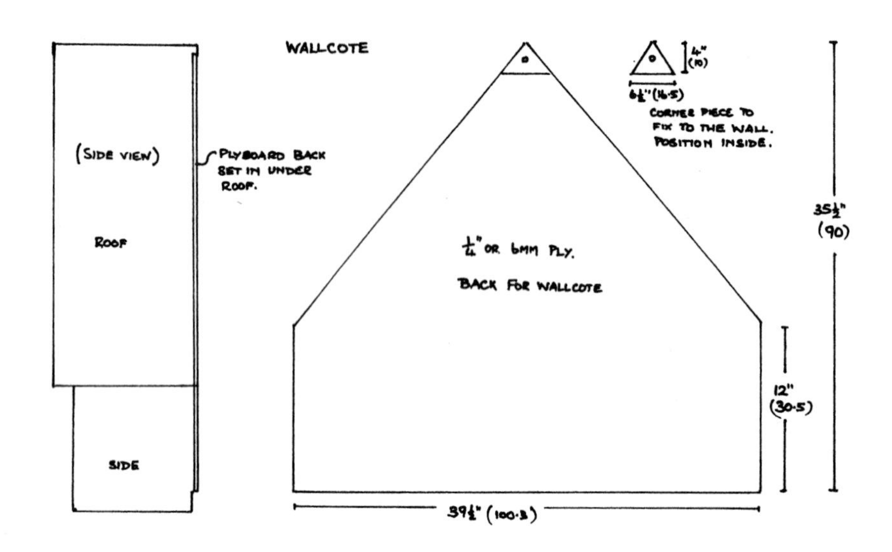
WALLCOTE
(SIDE VIEW)
ROOF
SIDE
PLYBOARD BACK SET IN UNDER ROOF.
¼" OR 6MM PLY.
BACK FOR WALLCOTE
4" (10)
6½" (16.5)
CORNER PIECE TO FIX TO THE WALL. POSITION INSIDE.
35½" (90)
12" (30.5)
39½" (100.3)

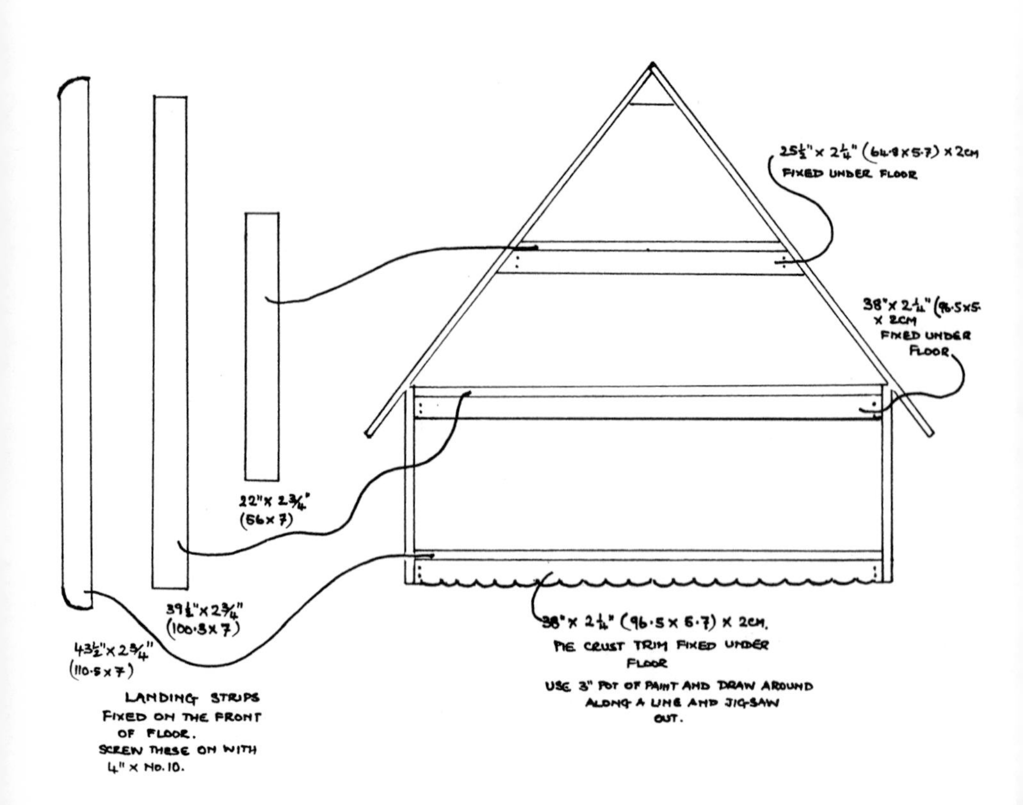
25½" x 2¼" (64.8 x 5.7) x 2CM
FIXED UNDER FLOOR
38" x 2¼" (96.5 x 5. x 2CM
FIXED UNDER FLOOR
22" x 2¾" (56 x 7)
39½" x 2¾" (100.3 x 7)
43½" x 2¾" (110.5 x 7)
38" x 2¼" (96.5 x 5.7) x 2CM.
PIE CRUST TRIM FIXED UNDER FLOOR
USE 3" POT OF PAINT AND DRAW AROUND ALONG A LINE AND JIG-SAW OUT.
LANDING STRIPS FIXED ON THE FRONT OF FLOOR.
SCREW THESE ON WITH 4" x No. 10.

WALLCOTE (NEST BOXES)

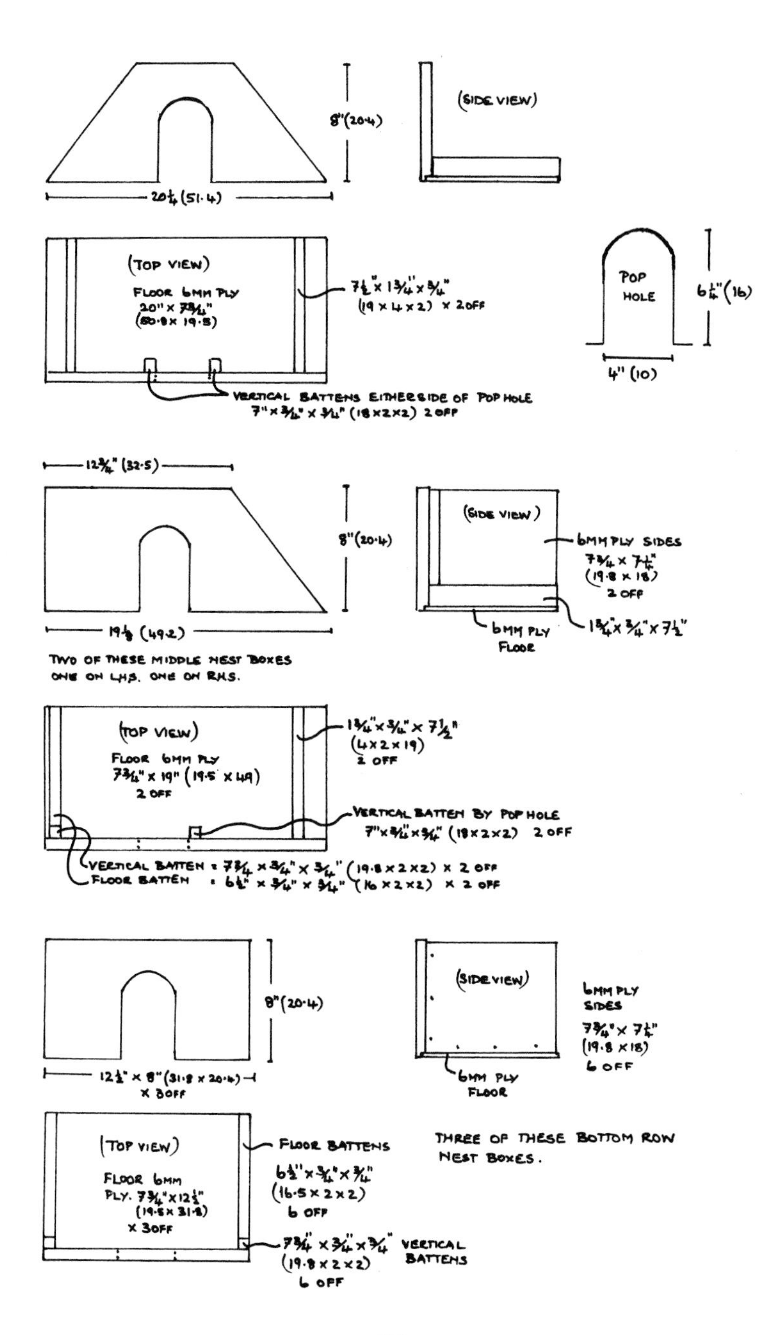

POLECOTE

I have studied the construction of polecotes for some time, and have found them to be unnecessarily fussy in design, mainly I think because people want them purely as decorative features in their gardens and need them to be as light as possible for transport and erection.

A very important aspect to consider is the management of the pigeons or doves in the polecote, which would not be easy perched up a ladder 8 feet off the ground; so I came up with the idea of having the accomodation part of the polecote on a winch so it can be lowered to waist height for easy management and no ladders.

I knew the house would be quite heavy, so in order to make it manageable, I constructed it in two halves to slide around a 4"x 4" square metal tube. Once offered up to the square tube, the two halves were bolted together while the roof remained fixed to the top of the post. This system works well, and our doves have been breeding in it happily for some months now; let's hope it will eventually lead to an improvement in the design of polecotes.

Make up the floor segments first, using the nest box dividers to hold the timber together. Remember that four of these have dividers both sides. You can diagonal nail the boards together on the ends. Drill in the wire cable holes then make up the central slides and fit the floors. Next fit the plyboard nest box dividers, and you will find the whole construction starting to pull together. Cut the sides and jig saw out the pop holes; start to add in the sides and make up the centre panels with their hinges. Make sure that all the sides are level at the top then screw these through to the floor segments. Use plated screws and hinges as they don't discolour the timber. Now add in the internal sheets (30" x 15.75") and you should have two halves made up. Don't forget to put the turn buttons on the inside of the opening side panels, just above the middle pop hole.

The roof is made all in one piece and is placed on the pole at the point of erection; the wire cables must be in place and hanging loose at this point as well. To make the roof, first cut out the two halves of its base then cut out the square hole in the middle for the central pole. Next cut the notches on each corner for the diagonal supports and fix on the perimeter pieces (1.5" x 1" x 26") between the notches. Chamfer these with a plane then fix in the lateral pieces to hold the base together. Put the base on top of the two joined halves of the accomodation section. Now put two pieces of 4" x 2" together to make a temporary central pole on which to build your roof, and slide it down through the central square hole. There should be approximately 33" poking out of the top above the base of the roof. Screw the top piece temporarily to this pole and start to add in the diagonal supports; these will need to be cut at an angle to meet the flat face of the top piece. Screw these up top and bottom then add the chamfered side bars onto the diagonal supports. Next fix the triangular roof pieces so that they fit flush with the supports; glue these and screw them down. You will notice a gap by the top piece; don't worry, this will be covered by the top cap which is made of thin galvanised or aluminium sheeting.

At this stage sandpaper and fill any cracks and apply primer and undercoat. Take your time over this as it needs to be a first class job. Now add on the top cap, folding the flaps or petals down carefully and screwing or nailing them flush onto the roof. Paint again with undercoat. Next add in the weather strips and undercoat those. It is as well to use two top coats to make a good job of it, as remember, once it is 12 feet up in the air it is

going to be difficult to get at! As soon as the roof is dry you will need two people to lift it off its temporary pole.

The metal work will have to be done by a local blacksmith or steel fabricator, and the metal pole will require painting before being concreted into the ground. Once the central pole is in, allow three days for the concrete to dry then screw the polecote accomodation brackets onto the metal riser. Now join the two halves of the accomodation together with two metal plates at the top, and screw the two floors onto the brackets. Thread the wire cables through the floors and attach them to the metal riser, making sure that they are both equally taut. The accomodation should slide up and down the pole and lock up under the roof with the ratchet system. One further point, you will need some wooden fillets for the corners of the accomodation part to finish the job properly. Your next problem will be stopping your doves from producing a population explosion!

POLECOTE

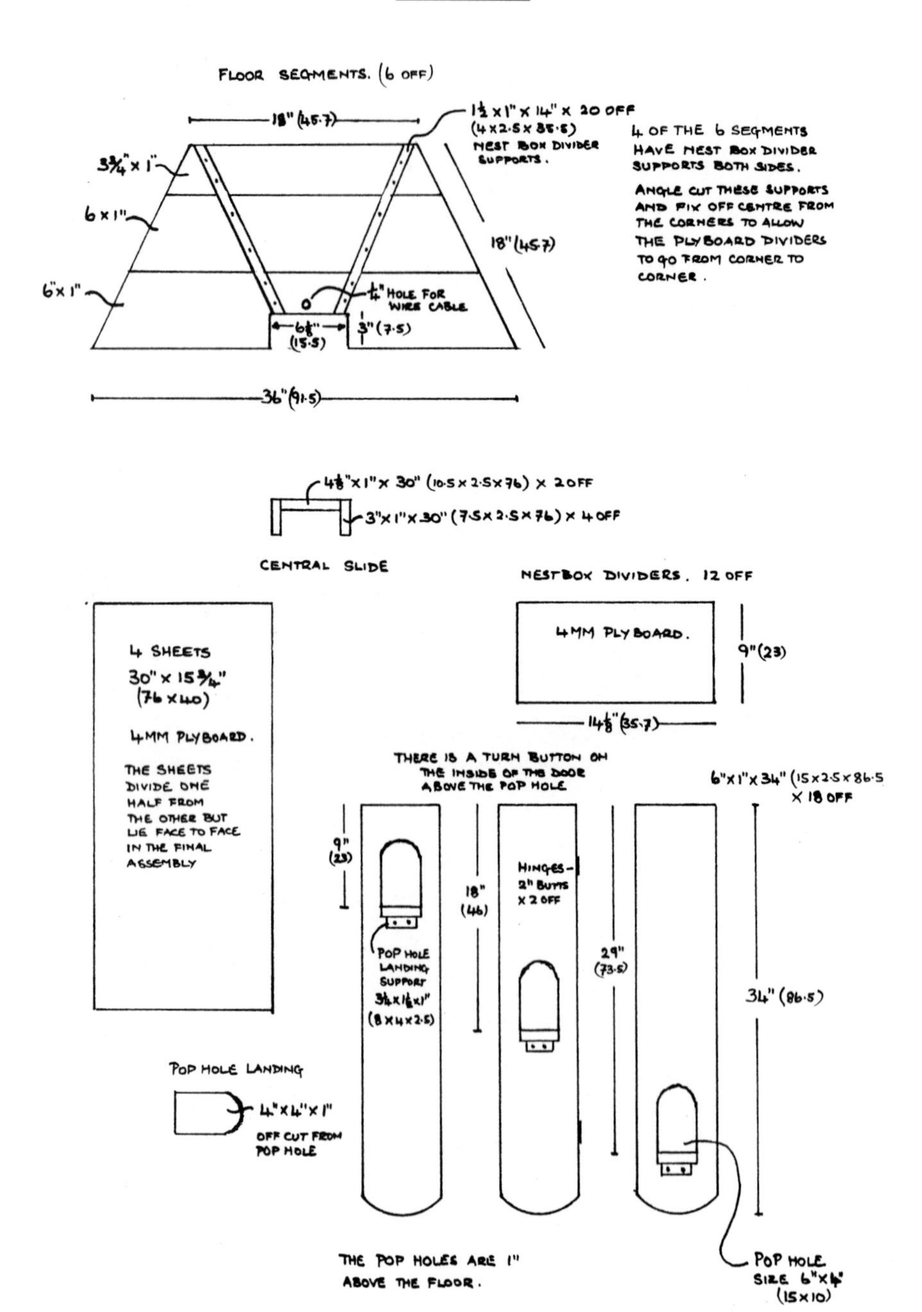

FLOOR SEGMENTS. (6 OFF)
18" (45.7)
1½ x 1" x 14" x 20 OFF
(4 x 2.5 x 35.5)
NEST BOX DIVIDER SUPPORTS.
4 OF THE 6 SEGMENTS HAVE NEST BOX DIVIDER SUPPORTS BOTH SIDES.
ANGLE CUT THESE SUPPORTS AND FIX OFF CENTRE FROM THE CORNERS TO ALLOW THE PLYBOARD DIVIDERS TO GO FROM CORNER TO CORNER.
3¾" x 1"
6 x 1"
6" x 1"
18" (45.7)
¼" HOLE FOR WIRE CABLE
6⅛" (15.5)
3" (7.5)
36" (91.5)
4⅛" x 1" x 30" (10.5 x 2.5 x 76) x 2OFF
3" x 1" x 30" (7.5 x 2.5 x 76) x 4 OFF
CENTRAL SLIDE
NESTBOX DIVIDERS. 12 OFF
4MM PLYBOARD.
9" (23)
14⅛" (35.7)
4 SHEETS
30" x 15¾" (76 x 40)
4MM PLYBOARD.
THE SHEETS DIVIDE ONE HALF FROM THE OTHER BUT LIE FACE TO FACE IN THE FINAL ASSEMBLY
THERE IS A TURN BUTTON ON THE INSIDE OF THE DOOR ABOVE THE POP HOLE
6" x 1" x 34" (15 x 2.5 x 86.5 x 18 OFF
9" (23)
18" (46)
HINGES - 2" BUTTS x 2 OFF
29" (73.5)
34" (86.5)
POP HOLE LANDING SUPPORT 3¼ x 1½ x 1" (8 x 4 x 2.5)
POP HOLE LANDING
4" x 4" x 1"
OFF CUT FROM POP HOLE
THE POP HOLES ARE 1" ABOVE THE FLOOR.
POP HOLE SIZE 6" x 4" (15 x 10)

POLECOTE

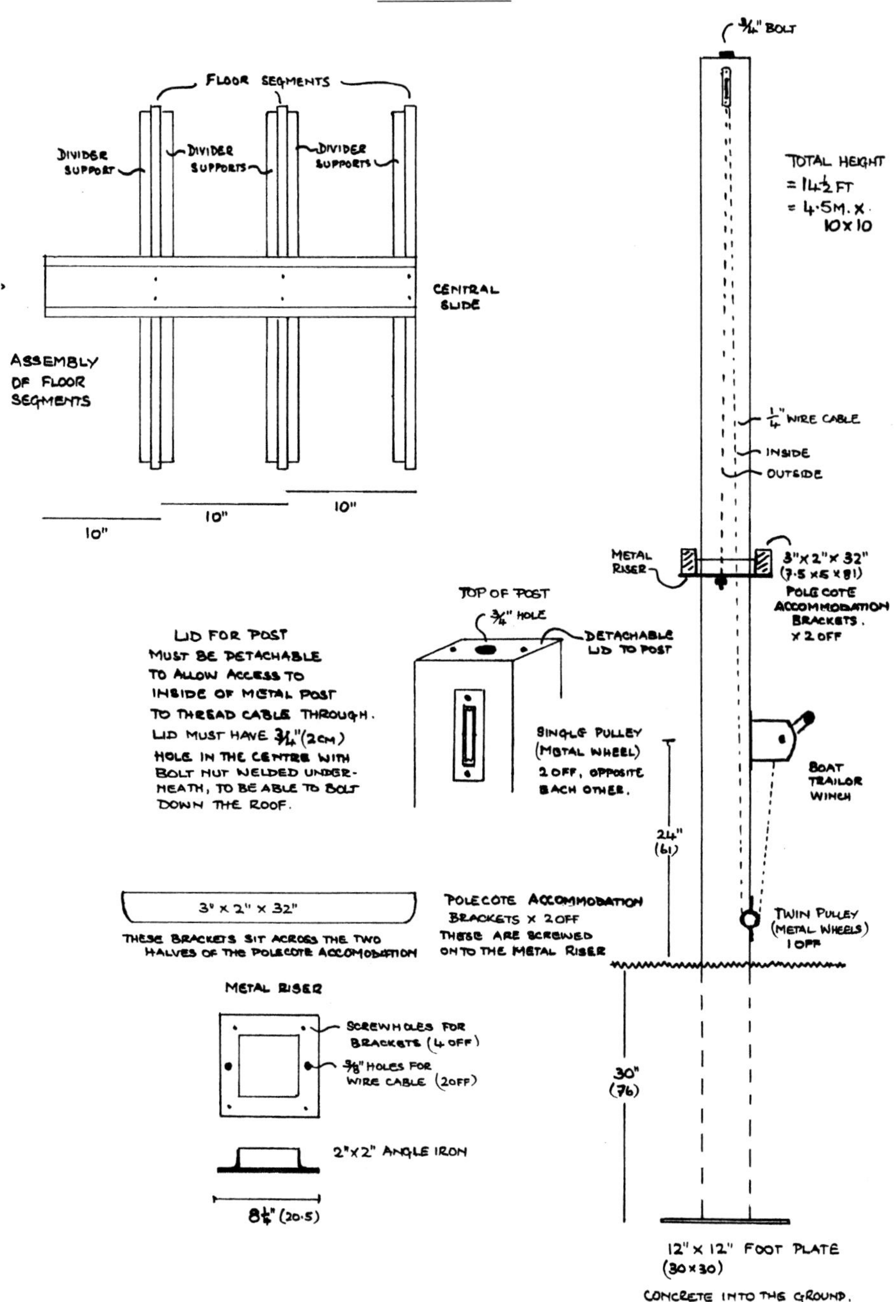

FLOOR SEGMENTS
DIVIDER SUPPORT
DIVIDER SUPPORTS
DIVIDER SUPPORTS
CENTRAL SLIDE
ASSEMBLY OF FLOOR SEGMENTS
10"
10"
10"
¾" BOLT
TOTAL HEIGHT = 14½ FT = 4·5M. x 10x10
¼" WIRE CABLE
INSIDE
OUTSIDE
METAL RISER
3"x 2"x 32" (7·5 x 5 x 81)
POLE COTE ACCOMMODATION BRACKETS. x 2 OFF
TOP OF POST
¾" HOLE
DETACHABLE LID TO POST
LID FOR POST
MUST BE DETACHABLE TO ALLOW ACCESS TO INSIDE OF METAL POST TO THREAD CABLE THROUGH. LID MUST HAVE ¾"(2CM) HOLE IN THE CENTRE WITH BOLT NUT WELDED UNDERNEATH, TO BE ABLE TO BOLT DOWN THE ROOF.
SINGLE PULLEY (METAL WHEEL) 2 OFF, OPPOSITE EACH OTHER.
BOAT TRAILOR WINCH
24" (61)
3" x 2" x 32"
THESE BRACKETS SIT ACROSS THE TWO HALVES OF THE POLECOTE ACCOMODATION
POLECOTE ACCOMMODATION BRACKETS x 2 OFF
THESE ARE SCREWED ONTO THE METAL RISER
TWIN PULLEY (METAL WHEELS) 1 OFF
METAL RISER
SCREWHOLES FOR BRACKETS (4 OFF)
⅜" HOLES FOR WIRE CABLE (2 OFF)
2"x2" ANGLE IRON
8½" (20·5)
30" (76)
12" x 12" FOOT PLATE (30 x 30)
CONCRETE INTO THE GROUND.

POLECOTE

THE ROOF OF THE POLECOTE IS MADE IN ONE PIECE AND IS BOLTED DOWN FROM THE TOP.

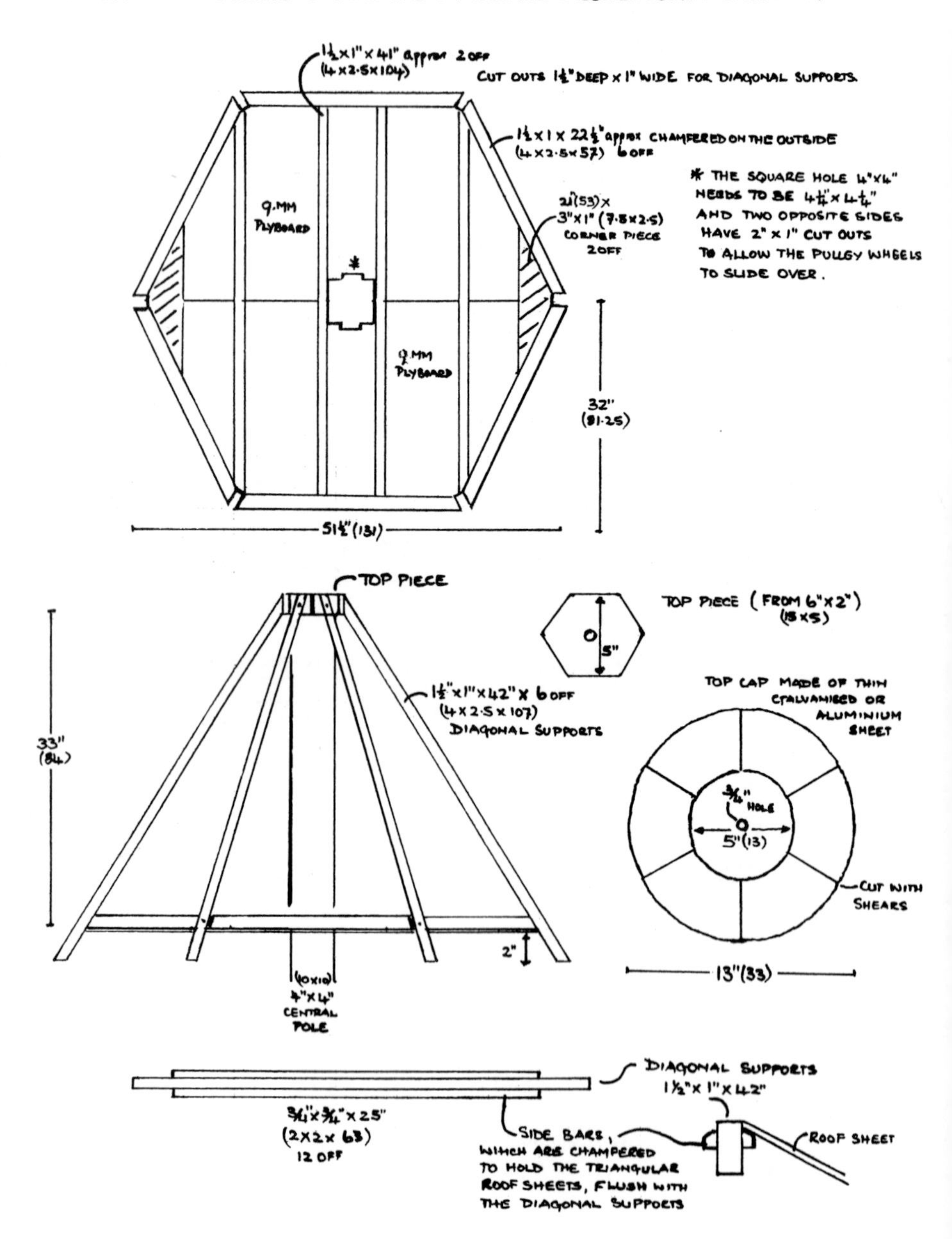

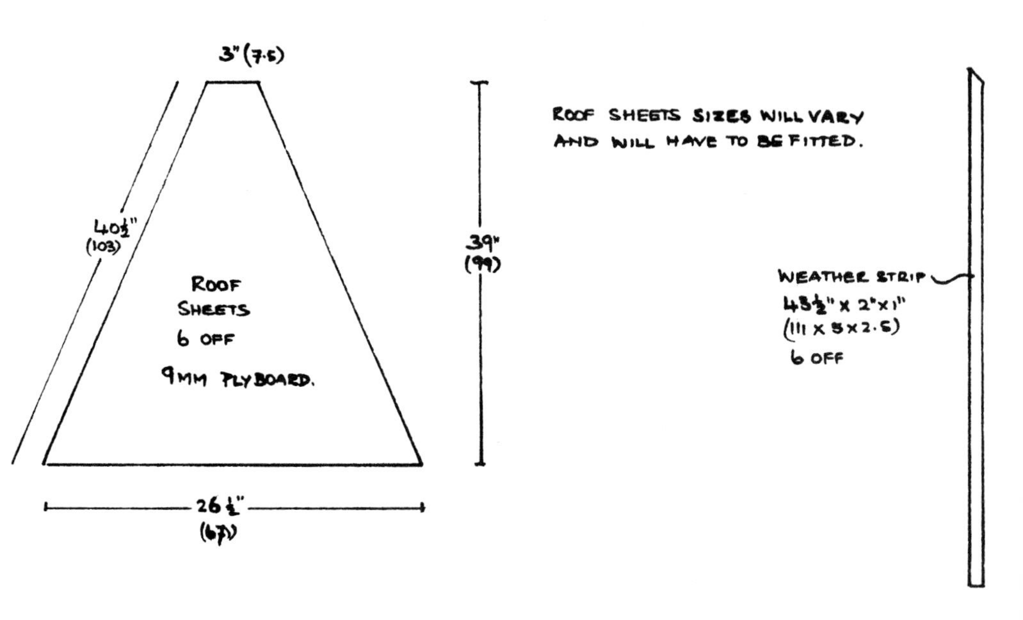
3" (7.5)
40½"
(103)
ROOF
SHEETS
6 OFF
9MM PLYBOARD.
39"
(99)
26½"
(67)
ROOF SHEETS SIZES WILL VARY
AND WILL HAVE TO BE FITTED.
WEATHER STRIP
43½" x 2" x 1"
(111 x 5 x 2.5)
6 OFF

GARDEN FENCE

I have produced two types of garden fence which can vary in the height you want them and the design. Most of these types of fence are used either at the front of the house against the road or as a division between the flower garden and the vegetable garden. They may also be used to keep small dogs from straying where they are not wanted.

When making this type of fence, care should be taken to ensure that the palings (uprights) remain vertical to the horizontal bars. Cut out the timber to size and place the two horizontals on the floor. Start at one end with one upright, and at the other end, just tack on another upright, making sure that it is at 90º to the horizontal and that the top and bottom are equal distances from the first upright. Now tack a straight board or a piece of 2"x 2" to the bottom end of the two uprights; this will ensure that all the palings are the same height. I have used 3" gaps between the palings, but you can choose the measurements and proportions you want. Now start fixing the uprights, using two 3" wide blocks as spacers, (or a measurement to suit youself). Every now and then check that the uprights are at 90º to the horizontal and that the tops and bottoms are equidistant from the first one. Adjust if necessary.

The posts that hold up this type of fencing must be 2 yards or 2 metres apart, so this is where you join the horizontals and cover the join with an upright so that the fencing looks continuous.

For fixing, you can either screw in from behind, ie drill the horizontal and screw through to the upright, or use a small head nail from the front. If you think that the fence might be vulnerable to vandalism, use a flat nail long enough to go through the paling and the horizontal and out the other side, then bend the end of the nail back flat against the horizontal. Providing the uprights are 1" thick, this makes a very sturdy fence.

The tops of the palings can be cut into various designs, but this depends on your ability and the time you can afford to spend on the job.

If you are going to paint the fence afterwards then rub down the palings and framework before screwing or nailing them together.

GARDEN FENCE (A)

MADE OF 3" x 1" (7.5 x 2.5)

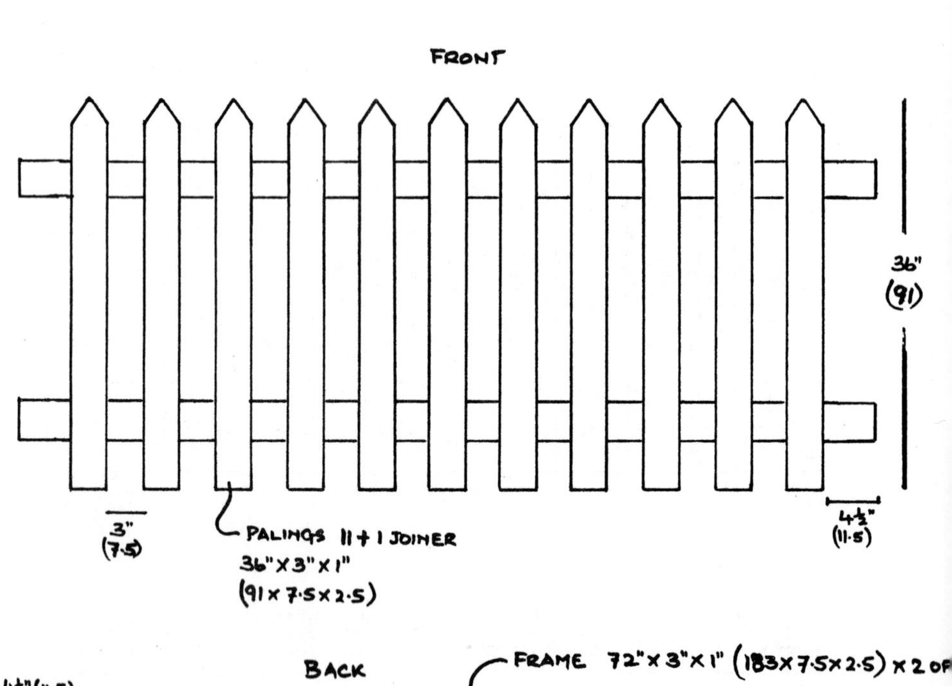

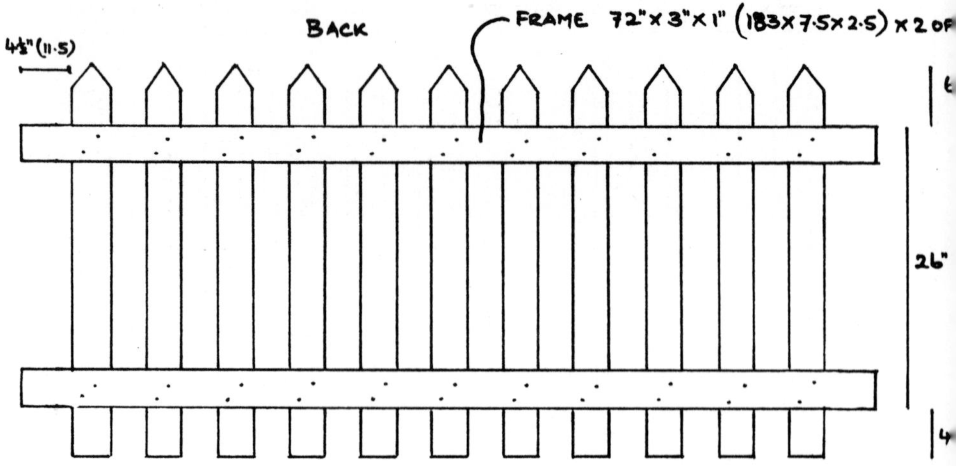

GARDEN FENCE (B)

MADE OF 3" x 1" (7.5 x 2.5)

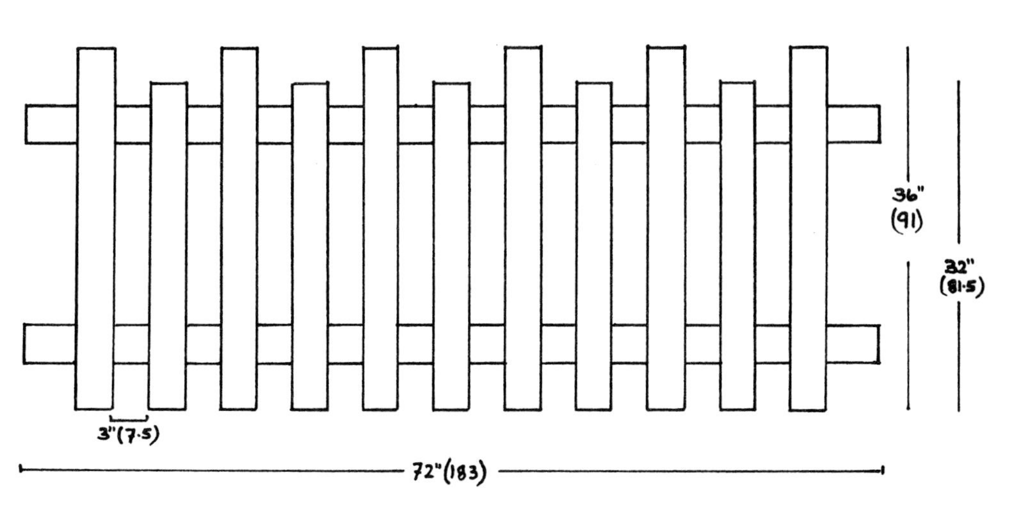

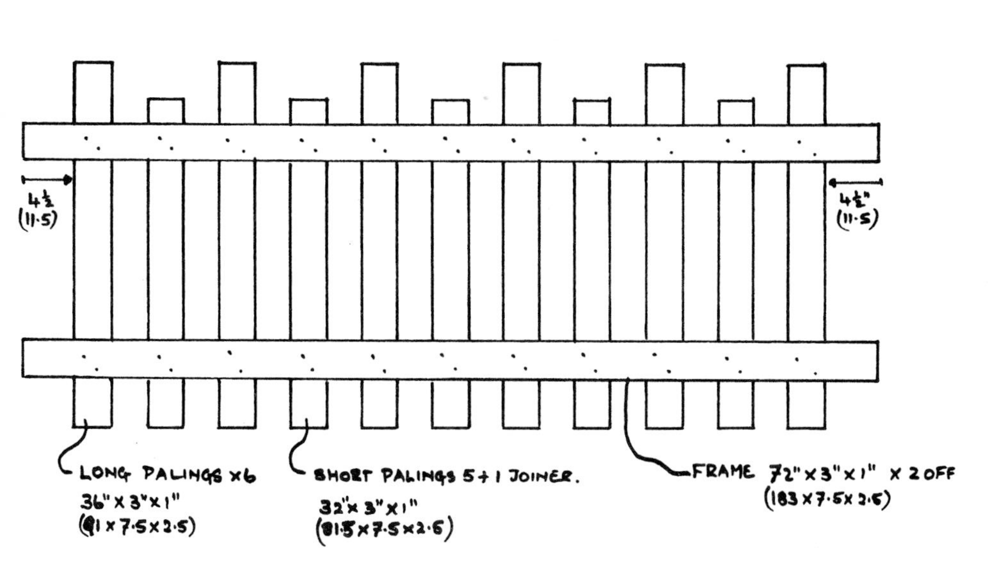

GARDEN GATE

This is similar to the garden fence in design and construction, but requires a diagonal piece the same size and thickness as the horizontals to stop the gate from sagging. The gate can be made to fit an existing opening, but it is advisable not to go any larger than 4 feet wide. Most people make their gates 3 feet wide which leaves enough room to push a wheelbarrow through without scraping your knuckles.

There are two types of hinge for this gate, hook and band which will allow the gate to be taken off for painting or extra access, or large Tee hinges 14" or 16" long. There are several types of gate catch available from good ironmongers or DIY stores where you can choose what is best suited to your circumstances and pocket.

The most important point when making your gate is to ensure that your horizontals and verticals are exactly at right angles. You can fix using screws into the back of the gate, and I would recommend drilling the frame before fitting them; an alternative would be to use flat head nails which go through from the front and come out at the back where they are hammered down flat. This makes a very strong gate. If you want it to marry up with the same style of garden fence, make sure that the horizontals are 26" apart rather than 28".

GARDEN GATE

MADE OF 3" x 1" (7.5 x 2.5)

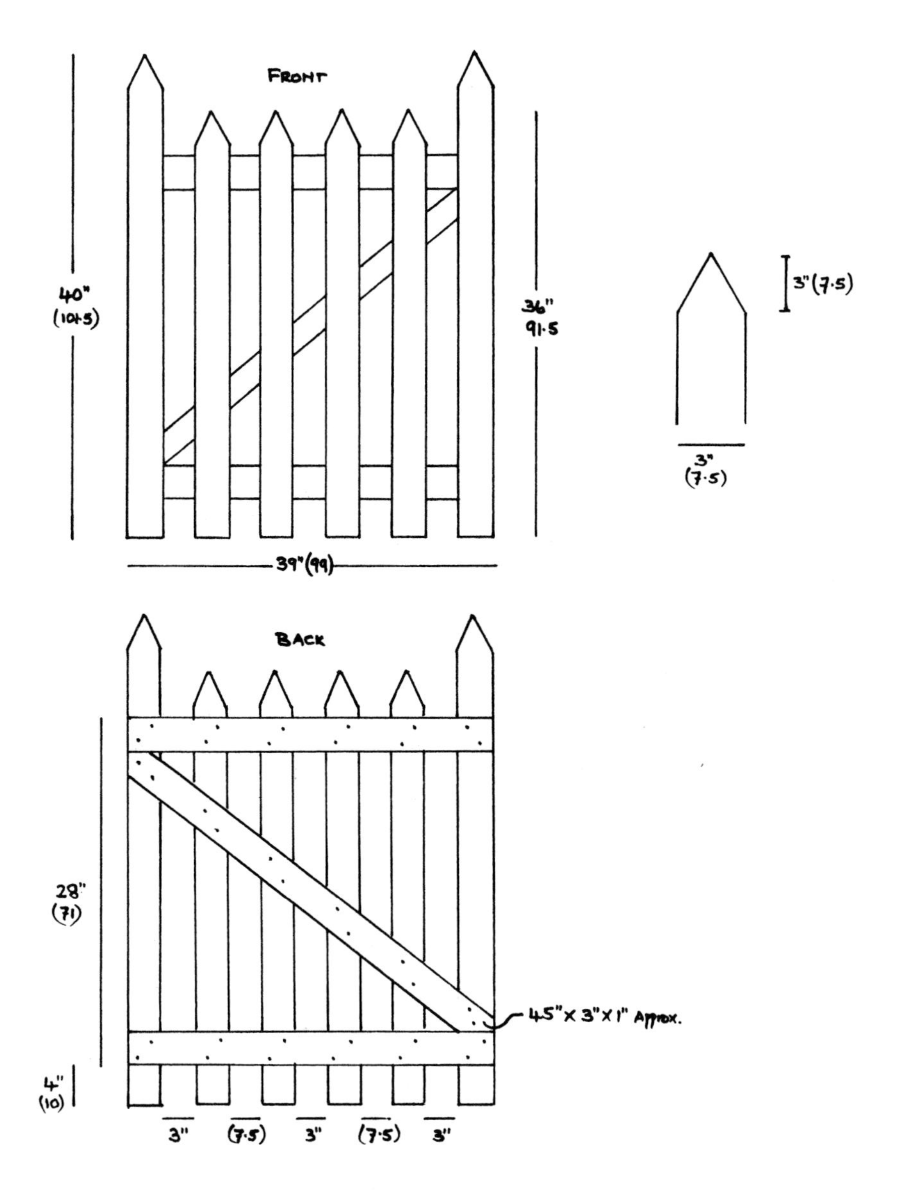

TRELLIS (LIGHT)

This was made for fixing to walls. It is lightweight but strong, is ideal for climbers such as clematis or jasmin etc. and is very quick to make. I have rawlplugged these to the wall of the house so that I can take them down when I want to paint the house.

This trellis is made of tiling batten or lath, 1.5" x 1" which is bench sawn down the middle. Only use timber that is free of knots, as otherwise the batten will break, and if you use galvanised screws, then predrill to avoid splitting the wood. I use 1.5" sherardised pins which work well. You will find this trellis rather flimsy until it is attached to a wall.

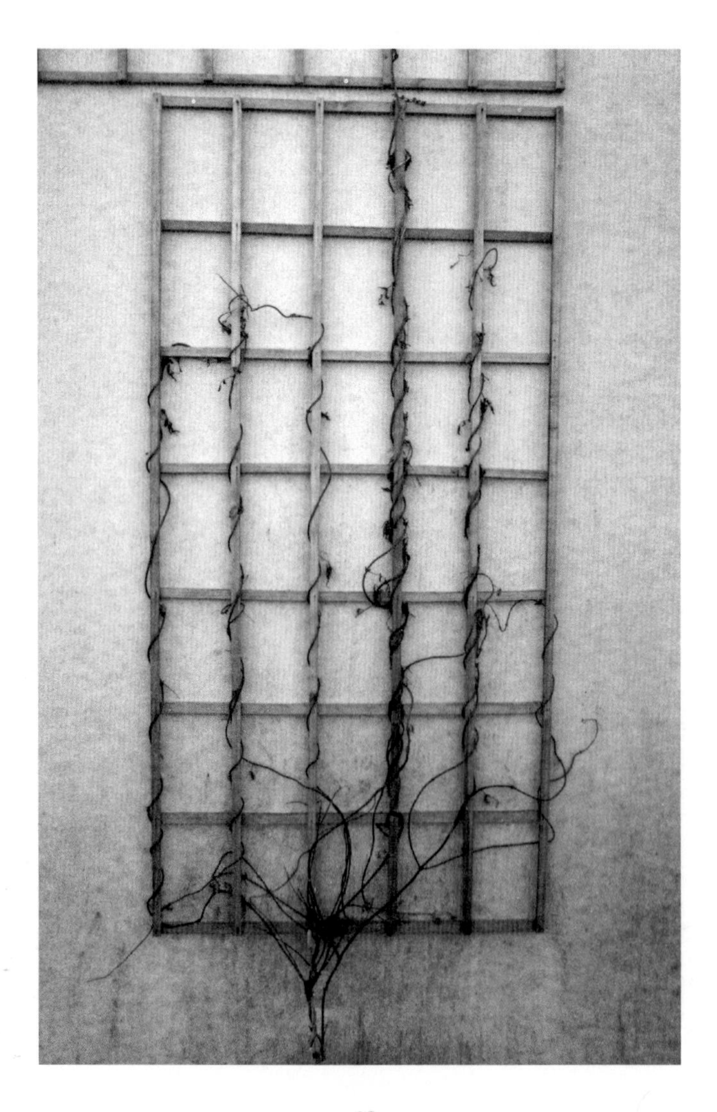

LIGHT TRELLIS

MADE OF 3/4" x 5/8" (2 x 1.5)

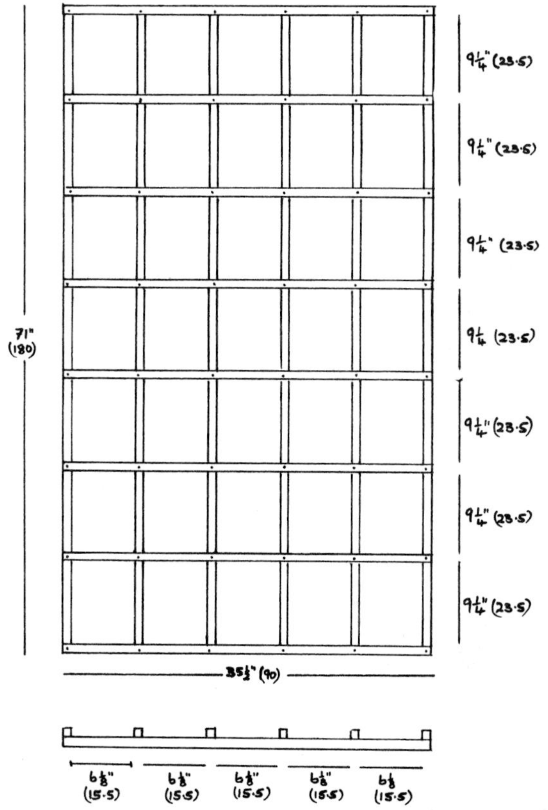

TRELLIS (DIAMOND)

This trellis comes in three different sections: the first has an entrance through, the second has a "window" in the middle and the third is plain. These can be put up in any combination to make a very attractive screen or divide between two parts of the garden. They are made of tanalised wood and can be stained or coated with a coloured wood preservative to prolong their outdoor life.

When making these, fix in the first diagonal, and using two blocks of wood 7" long as spacers, nail or screw in the rest. Check from time to time that the distances are always the same top and bottom.

Cut the timber and make up the frame for the plain trellis first. Turn the frame over and start to put in the diagonals, beginning with the longest. Once that is fitted, start to cut and nail in the other diagonals, using two 7" pieces of off-cut timber as spacers. When that is completed, turn the frame over and do the same on the other side, starting with the longest diagonal again and continuing as before. I use sherardised 1.5" (40 mm) pins to fit the diagonals together, and oval nails for the rest.

When making the window trellis, just jigsaw out the "window" carefully so that there are no rough edges showing.

The archway is a little more complicated. Cut and make up the frame and add in the archway, nailing a piece of wood temporarily along the bottom to hold it in place. Put the plain trellis alongside the archway one and start to work out the diamonds so that they match up with the plain trellis. Then, using the 7" spacers, start to fill in the diagonals so that they match both sides all the way up. Once tacked into position, nail them down permanently.

TRELLIS (DIAMOND) ENTRANCE

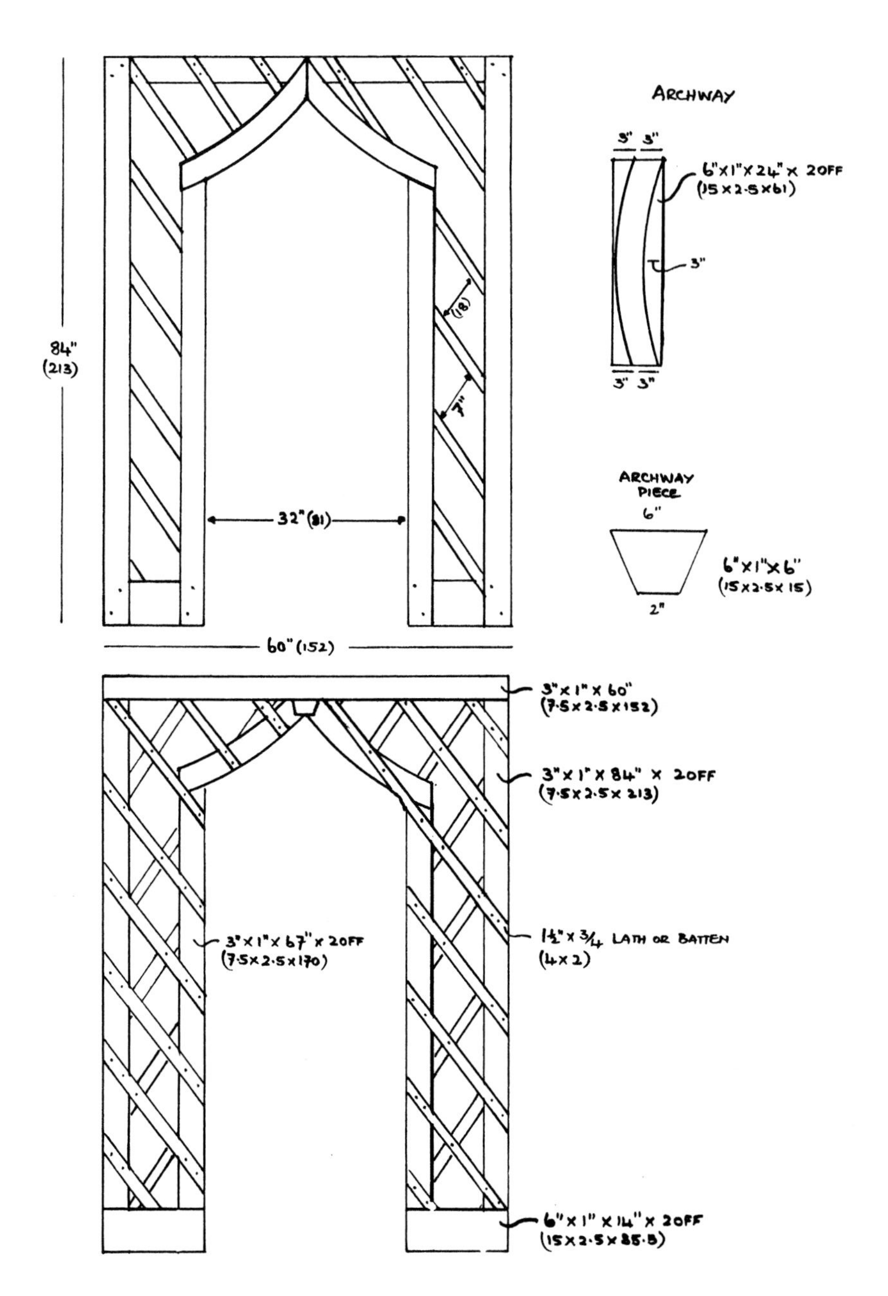

TRELLIS (DIAMOND) PLAIN

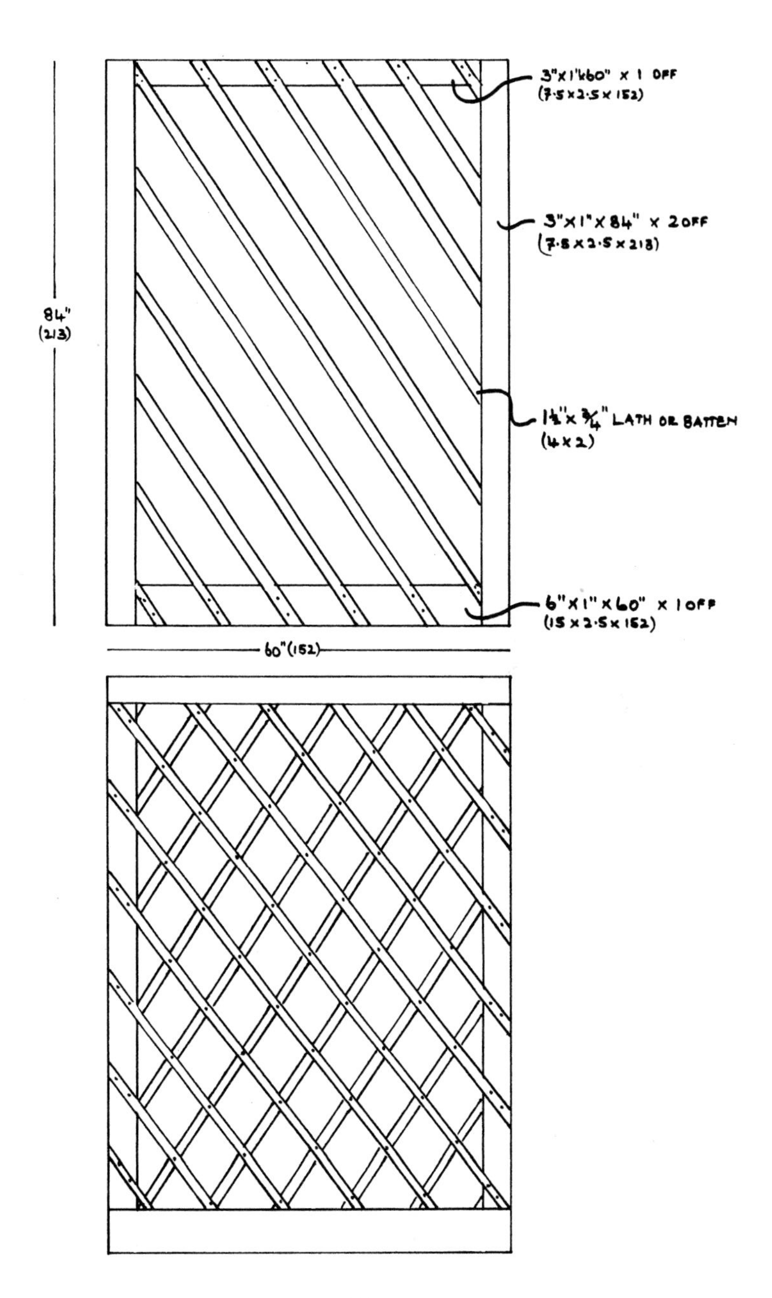

TRELLIS (DIAMOND) WINDOW

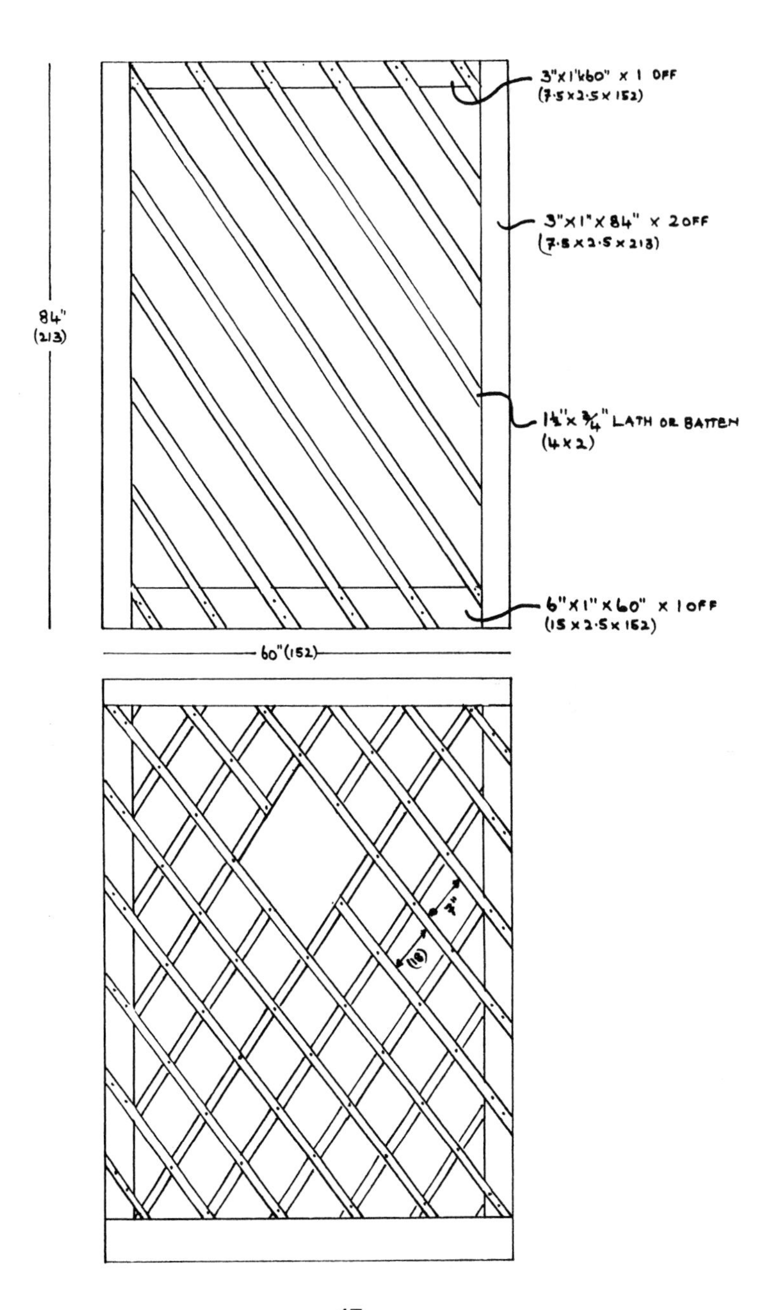

TRELLIS (HEAVY DUTY)

This trellis was designed to support heavy climbers like roses or honeysuckle etc. and there is the option of including a window as well. It is very easy to make, but the window has to be mitred and fitted into the uprights.

The trellis is made of tanalised wood, but it can be stained or painted with wood preservative.

Cut and make up the frame then add in the vertical bars and the cross bars. Now make the square piece with the mitred corners and offer it up to the trellis. Carefully mark the V cuts and jigsaw them out. You will need a small block with a V cut in it on the horizontal bar to hold the square in place.

HEAVY TRELLIS

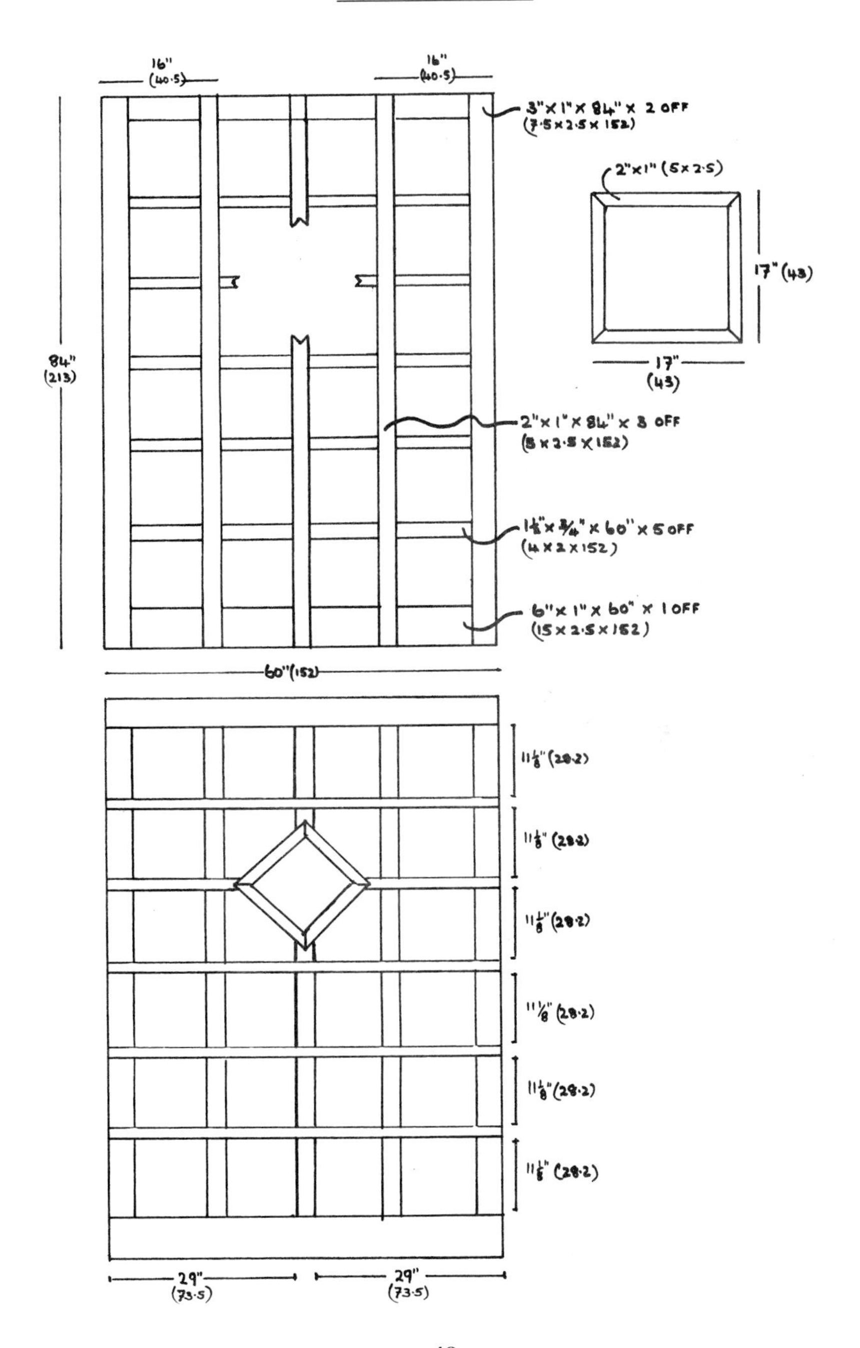

PLANTER (SMALL)

Whereas the large planter when filled with soil and plants is a very heavy lump to move, these small ones are easy and can be dotted about on terraces, steps and wooden decking to add splashes of colour when and where needed.

They are very easy to make as the sides are identical pairs fixed together. Care should be taken to jigsaw the floorboards around the corner sections which will give the construction more strength. Try to ensure that the mitred top lip is exact because if it is not you will notice this every time you water the plants in it!

SMALL PLANTER

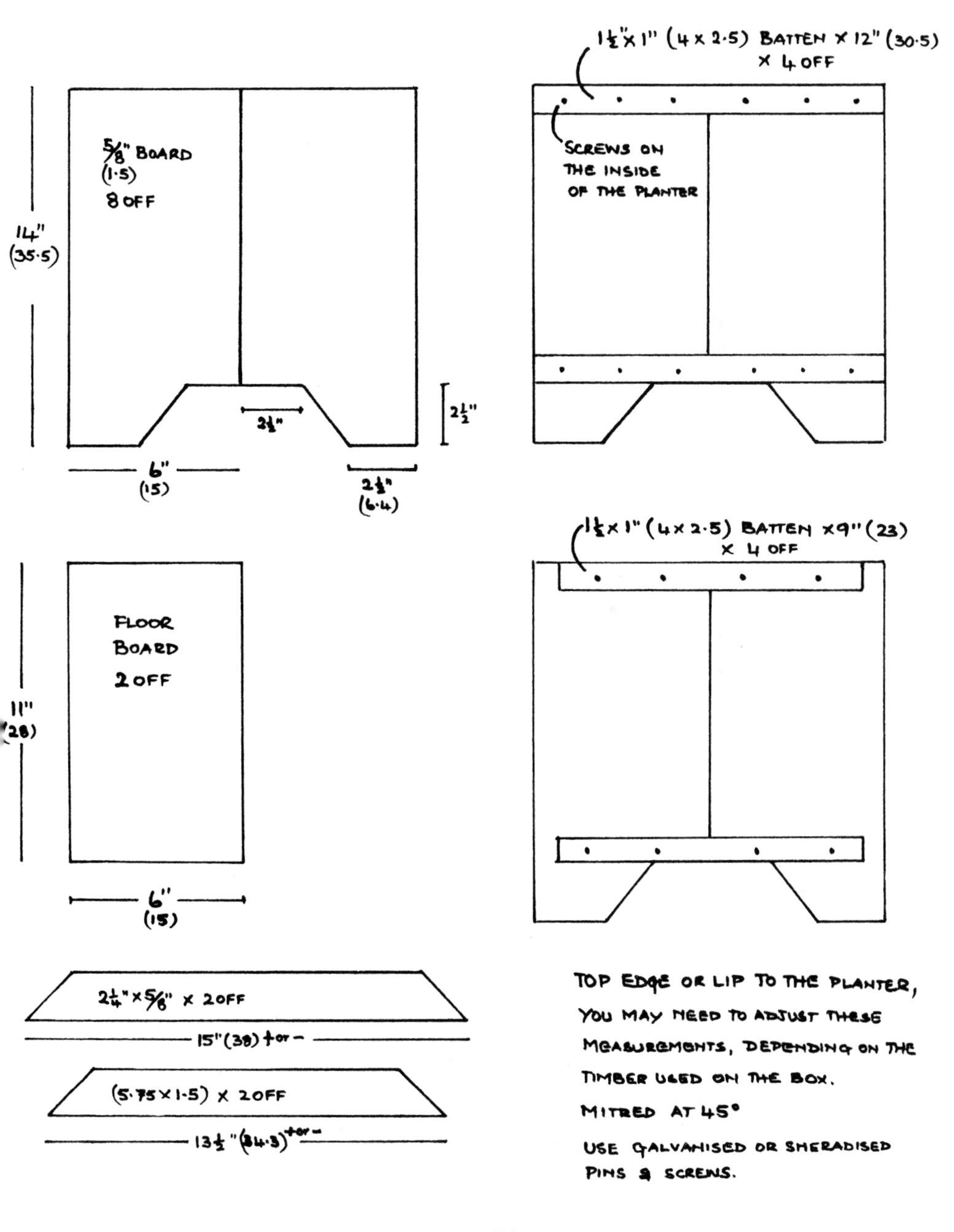

PLANTER (LARGE)

Planters are very useful in any garden as they can be placed strategically; they were originally used for tender plants which were over-wintered in large conservatories.

This design is very easy to make and very strong, and again I have made it of tanalised soft wood. The sides of the planter are two identical pairs which are held together by battens inside. The floor and the mitred top lip strengthen the construction.

Cut the twelve boards and jigsaw out the bottom cut-outs. Cut and fix the top and bottom battens. Bore the batten first and screw the sides up from the inside. Fit all the sides together and fix with screws and nails, then put in the floor boards and screw them to the bottom battens.

Now measure up the top edge or lip of the planter. Tack the lip to the top of the box all the way round; two sides will be on top of the other sides at the corners. Measure and cut the angle at 45 degrees exactly using an angle set square, and making sure that you are as precise as possible.

LARGE PLANTER

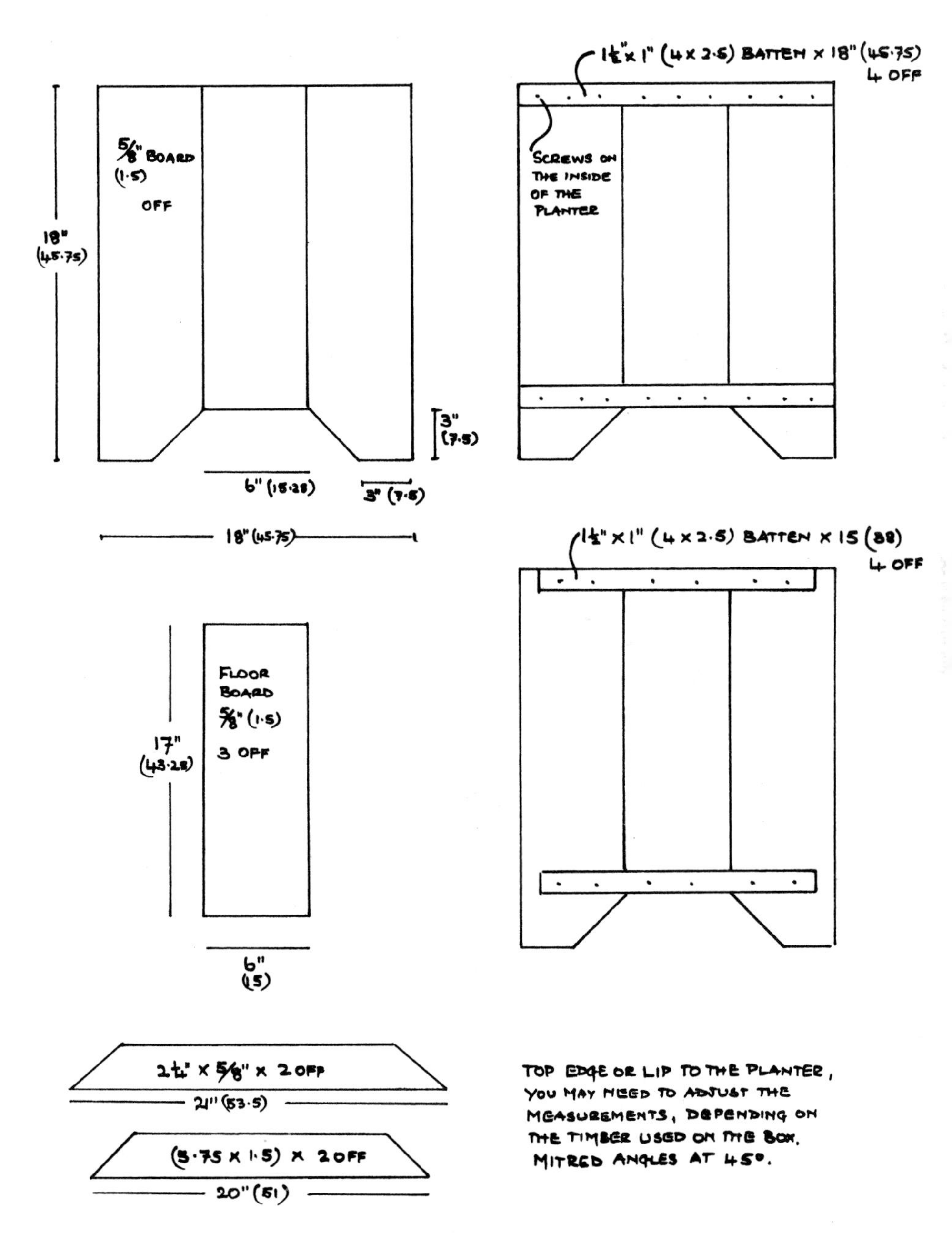

RAISED TROUGHS (LARGE & SMALL)

These troughs are particularly useful in two ways: first they are more convenient for the elderly who don't have to bend down so far to pick herbs from them for instance, and secondly they are too high for the aim of any passing dog or cat!

Cut the 22" long legs out of 3" x 2" and then make up the front, back and two side panels. To assemble the panels, drill each side piece twice (8.75" x 1.5" x 1") and screw into the leg. Remember to leave a 1" gap at the top. Once all the panels are in place, fit in the floor boards. Measure and cut them out exactly to ensure a good fit; take plenty of time and care when you do this, as the floor boards lock everything together. Screw the floor boards in.

I have lined my troughs with thick polythene sheeting to help retain water as they soon dry out in the summer. Conversely, however, they can become waterlogged if exposed to too much rain or a leaky gutter.

In some parts of England trough is pronounced "troh" instead of the usual "troff". The word trough comes from old English and always used to be pronounced "troh".

SMALL TROUGH

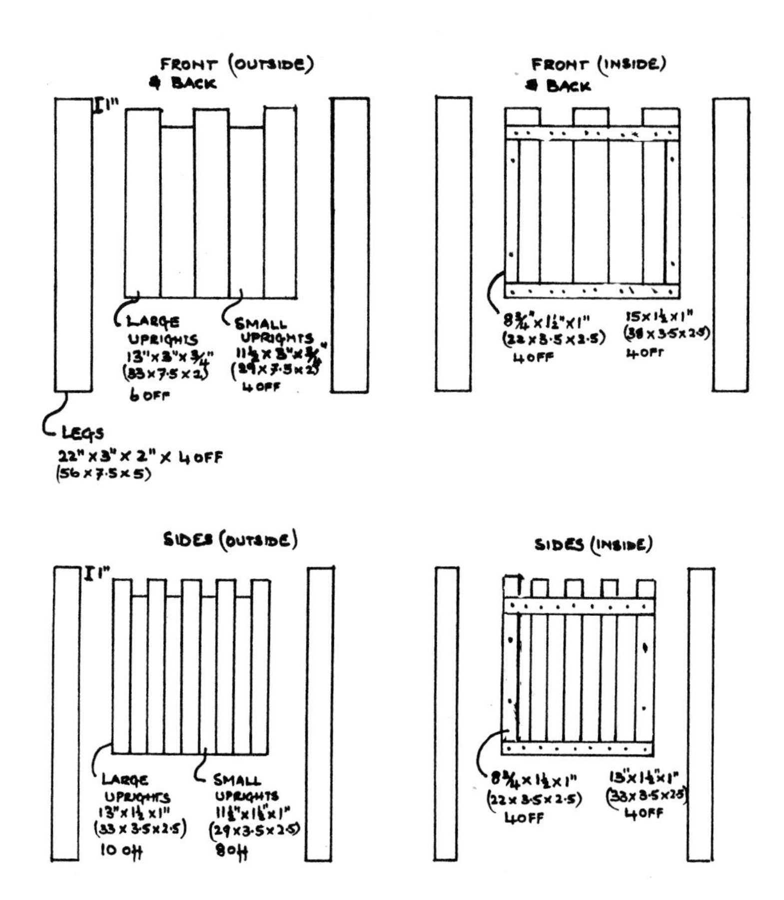

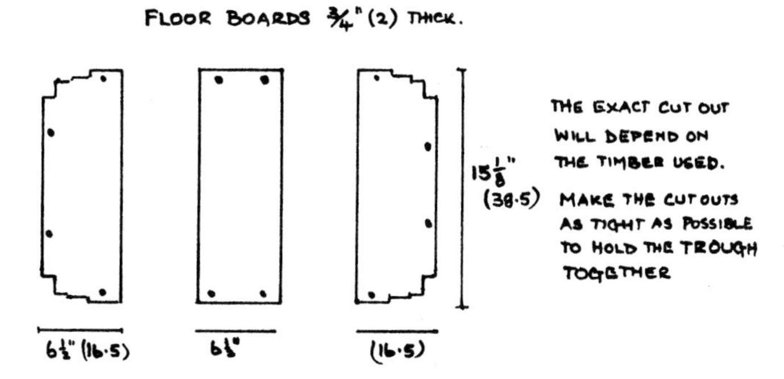

RAISED TROUGH (LARGE)

LARGE TROUGH

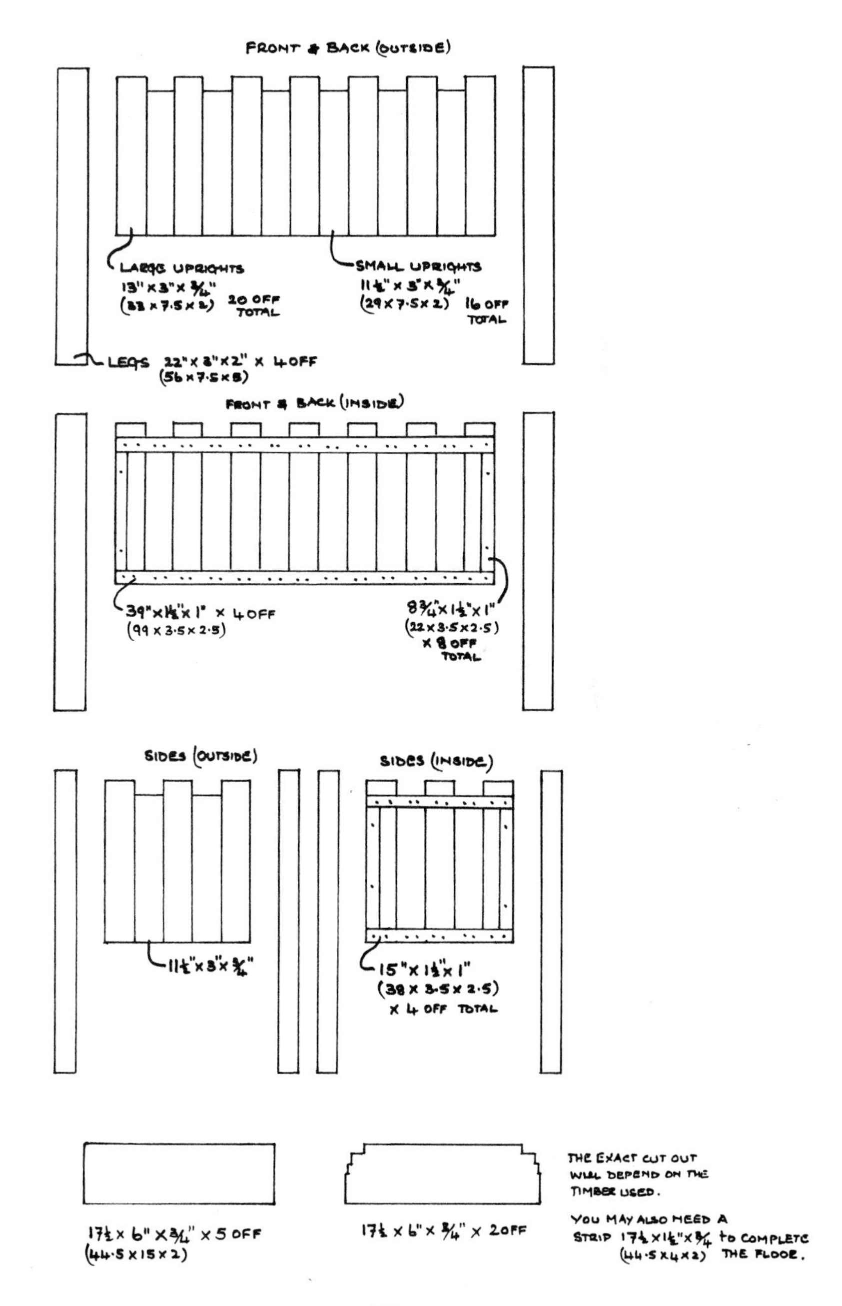

APPLE STORE

This not something that you can buy off the shelf, so I designed this store because we had a huge crop of Bramley apples and nowhere to keep them. I must confess this is still at the experimental stage, but we have got through to Easter without buying a cooking apple! Most stores encountered in country houses are part of brick or stone buildings which are marvellous for moderating temperatures and humidity

What I found myself making was a kind of incubator in reverse; I constructed the wooden closet with pull-out drawers, put wire mesh floors in the drawers and lined the mesh with newspaper. I fixed a bathroom extractor fan inside the top of the closet and timed it to come on for a quarter of an hour every night to remove any stale air and draw in cold air from floor level. I also thought this might remove many of the fungus spores that would be hanging about.

The jury is out as to the fine tuning of this apple store, but the construction may well receive some modification before the next apple season begins. I also think that there is quite a knack involved in knowing the right time to pick an apple.

I have this store set up in a timber building on a concrete floor; hard frosts are not common in this part of Devon.

Cut and make up the back panel then cut and make up the two side panels. I pinned the shelf bearers from inside and then screwed them in from outside as they do support some weight. Fix on the two pieces 2" x 1.5" x 50" to hold the front together. Now fix in the bottom front board 6" x 1" x 35" with the inspection cover and the top plyboard panel 35" x 9".

Make up the doors next; the right hand door has a cover strip 40" x 2" x 6mm plyboard. Fix in the two pieces 1.5" x 1" x 40" which will support the door hinges, then hang the doors and add the turn buttons; the bottom turn button will need a small block behind it.

The drawers are next. You will need a roll 1 metre wide and 10 metres long of medium gauge 1" x 1" weld mesh. Make up the eight 36" x 28" frames first and staple on the weldmesh, then add on the two 38.5" bearers and 27" central support. Make sure that all nails or screws are counter sunk so that the drawers slide in and out nicely.

I put newspaper on top of the weldmesh and then placed the apples in rows on the shelves, making sure that they were not touching each other.

APPLESTORE

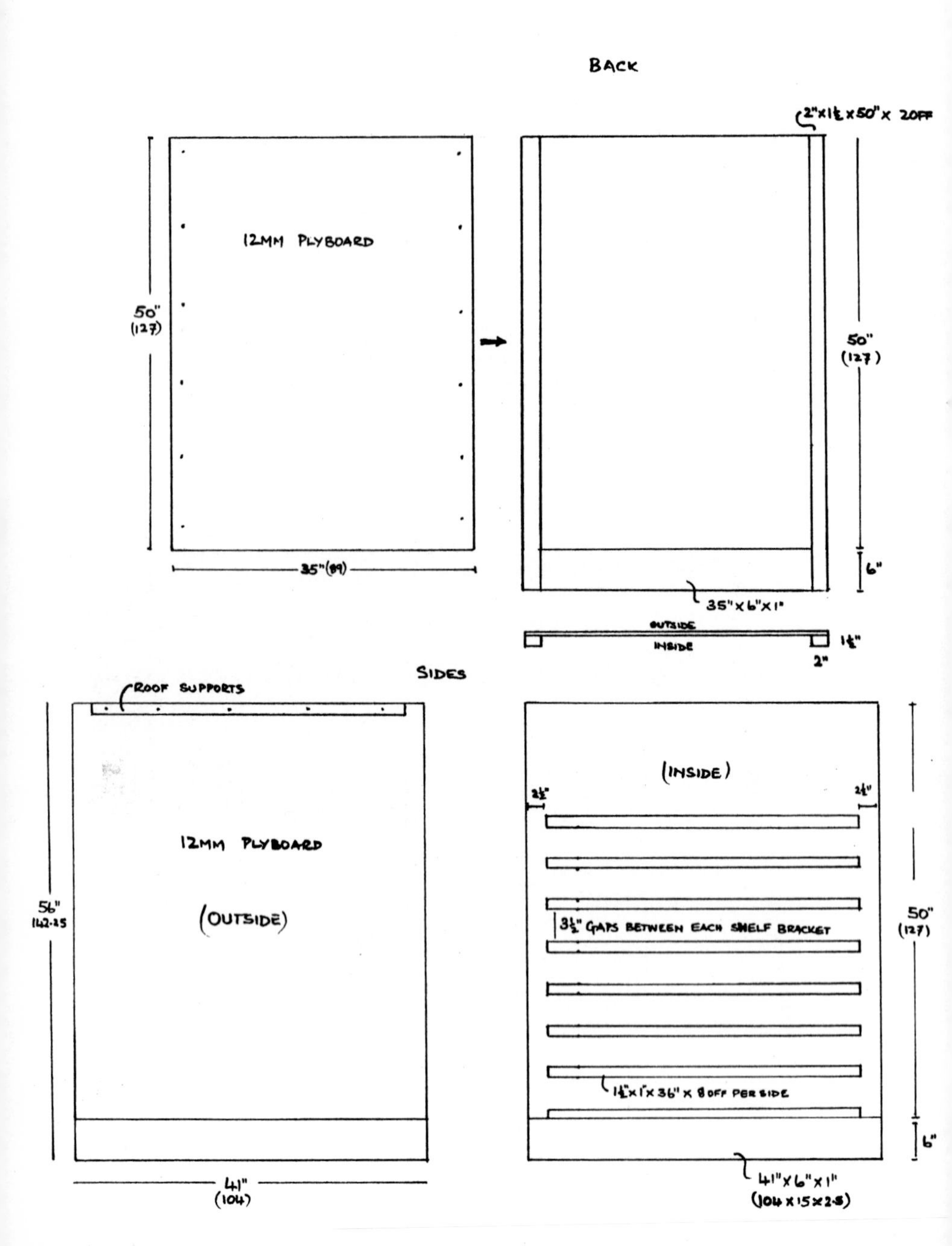
BACK
2"x1½x50"x 2OFF
12MM PLYBOARD
50" (127)
35"(89)
50" (127)
6"
35"x6"x1"
OUTSIDE
INSIDE
1½"
2"
SIDES
ROOF SUPPORTS
12MM PLYBOARD
(OUTSIDE)
56" 142·25
41" (104)
(INSIDE)
2½"
2½"
3½" GAPS BETWEEN EACH SHELF BRACKET
50" (127)
1½"x1"x 36" x 8 OFF PER SIDE
6"
41"x6"x1"
(104 x 15 x 2·5)

APPLESTORE

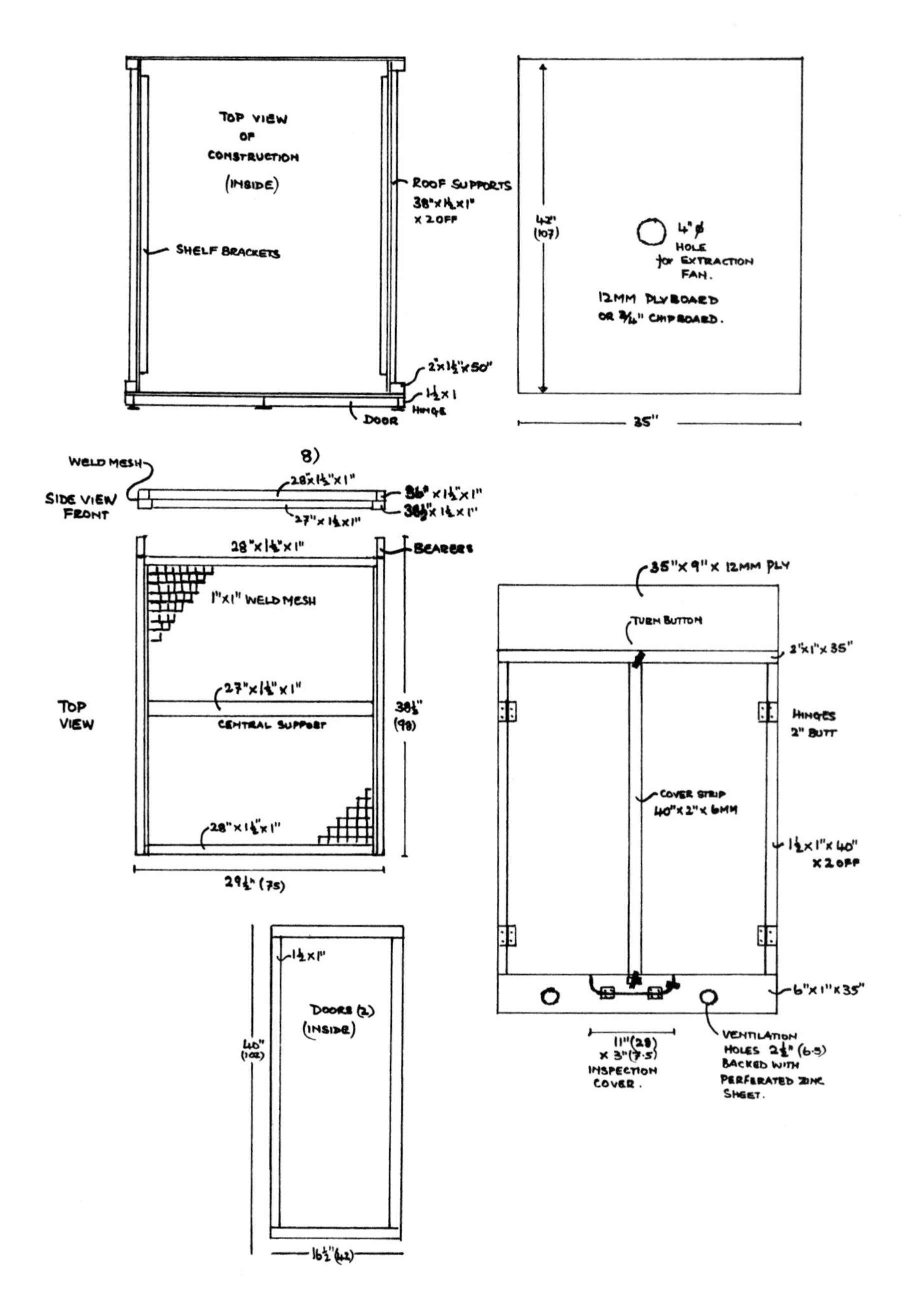

TOP VIEW OF CONSTRUCTION (INSIDE)
ROOF SUPPORTS 38"x1½x1" x 2OFF
SHELF BRACKETS
2"x1½"x50"
1½x1
HINGE
DOOR
42" (107)
4"ø HOLE for EXTRACTION FAN.
12MM PLYBOARD OR ¾" CHIPBOARD.
35"
8)
WELD MESH
SIDE VIEW FRONT
28"x1½"x1"
36"x1½"x1"
38½"x1½x1"
27"x1½x1"
28"x1½"x1"
BEARERS
1"x1" WELD MESH
TOP VIEW
27"x1½"x1"
CENTRAL SUPPORT
38½" (98)
28"x1½"x1"
29½" (75)
35"x9"x 12MM PLY
TURN BUTTON
2"x1"x35"
HINGES 2" BUTT
COVER STRIP 40"x2"x 6MM
1½x1"x40" x2OFF
1½x1"
DOORS (2) (INSIDE)
40" (102)
16½" (42)
6"x1"x35"
11"(28) x 3"(7.5) INSPECTION COVER.
VENTILATION HOLES 2½" (6.5) BACKED WITH PERFERATED ZINC SHEET.

NEST BOX

I have always been fascinated by the various designs of nest box and have often wondered how you cleaned them out. Most people don't realise the importance of cleaning nest boxes because of the build-up of red mite carried by wild birds; these mites can literally suck the blood of a young chick until it dies, so I was determined to design a nest box that was accessible for easy cleaning.

This one is very easy to make, and the entrance hole can be varied in size depending on the species you wish to attract.

At present I am using these in an oak wood, trying to attract pied flycatchers; last year four were used, but I didn't have time to look into which birds might have been the occupants, although the nesting material could have been that of a pied flycatcher.

I found that the most economic method of making these nest boxes was to construct them in batches of 6 or 8. Cut out the pieces from planks of 6" x 1" then nail or screw the sides, turn the box over and fix in the 1" x 1" x 6" floor support. Now add the roof, but use glue to fasten it to the sides and back. Make up the front and floor and drill out the hole size required. The landing strip which the wire goes through is cut out on the bench saw, just a simple groove. Glue and pin this then assemble the box and push the wire through the landing strip. Fasten with two half inch staples but don't push them right home otherwise you will not be able to withdraw the wire later. You may need to add a nail to clip the wire in.

BIRD NEST BOX

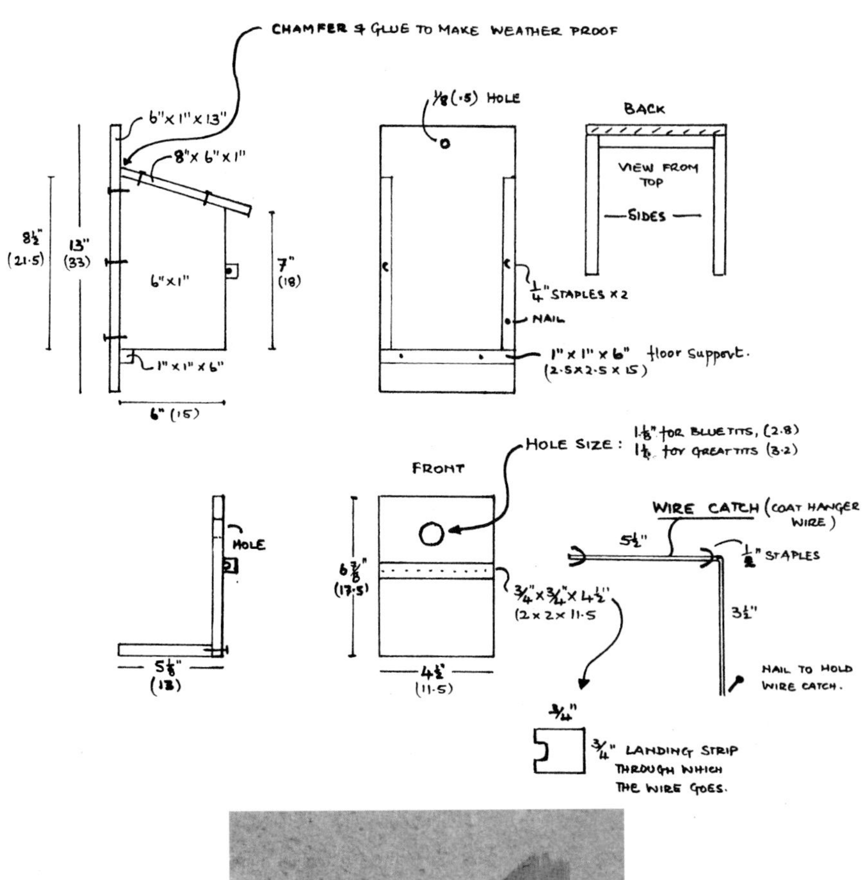

HOSE REEL

I wanted a hose reel that could take 50 plus yards or metres of hose, and that could wind on easily and still function with the hose on or partly off the reel.

Make up the base first, and then cut out the 5mm plyboard sides and drill out the centre 1.25" hole. Screw the sides onto the base from the inside at the bottom.

Jigsaw out the wooden spacers from 6" x 1" and drill the centre holes. Now drill with a 4 or 5mm bit from the side into the centre so that a 2" screw will lock onto the shaft. Cut out two round pieces for the drum, and with a compass make a circle of 3.75" (9.5mm) from the centre point. Drill holes round this line at 12 o'clock, 1.30, 3.00, 4.30, 6.00, 7.30, 9.00, and 10.30, (8 in all) to fix the centre pieces of the drum; also drill the centre 1.25" hole. Assemble the drum and put two screws into each of the centre pieces to stop them from rotating. The shaft is a 1.25" broom handle, and I have used 5" (13mm) off-cuts from it as handles which are screwed onto the handle bar from the back; I have made two of these for my hose reel but this is not necessary.

Screw the wooden spacers onto the drum and assemble onto the wooden sides, and then slide the shaft through; this might be a tight fit. Cut the shaft carefully and add on the handle bar. Screw up the retaining screws on the wooden spacers with a long handled screwdriver and drill the 4mm hole through the handlebar and shaft. Put the bolt through and tighten it up.

HOSE REEL

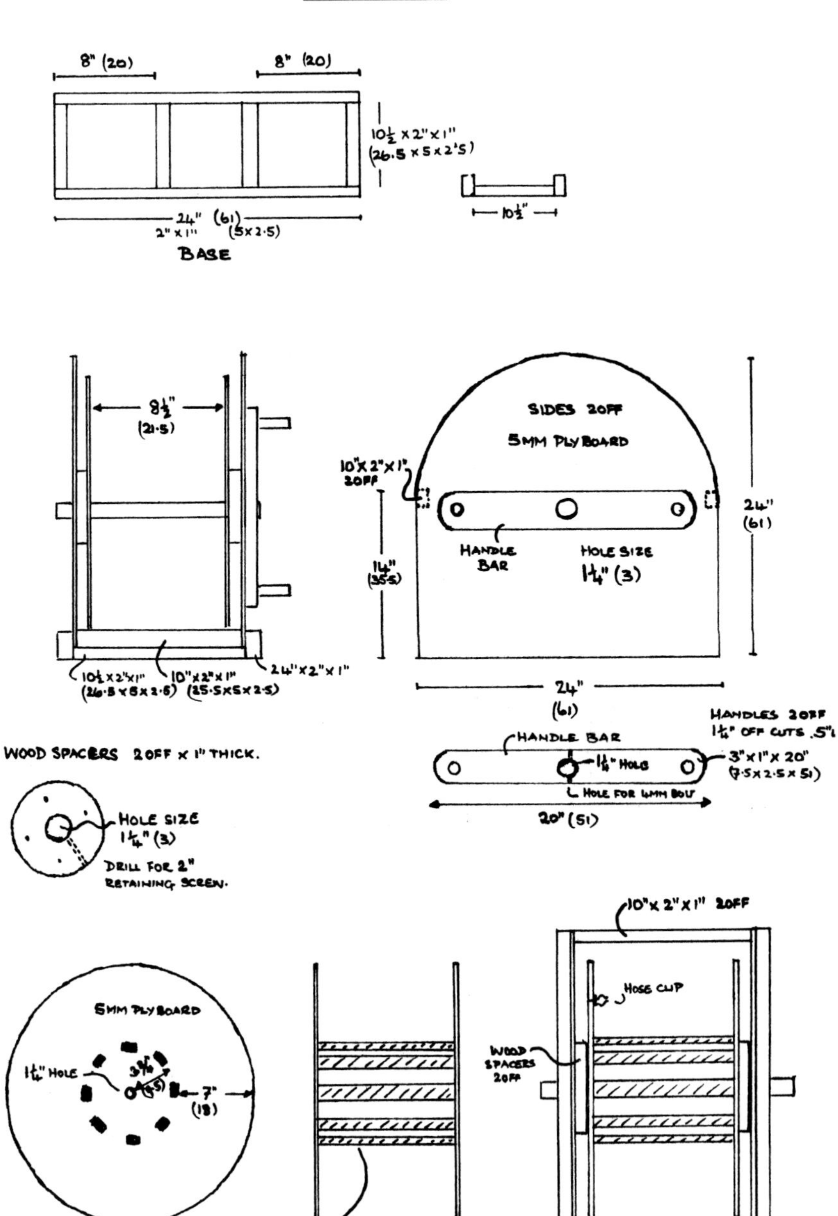

8" (20)
8" (20)
10½ x 2" x 1"
(26.5 x 5 x 2.5)
24" (61)
2" x 1" (5 x 2.5)
BASE
10½"
8½"
(21.5)
10½ x 2" x 1"
(26.5 x 5 x 2.5)
10" x 2" x 1"
(25.5 x 5 x 2.5)
24" x 2" x 1"
SIDES 2OFF
5MM PLYBOARD
10" x 2" x 1"
2OFF
HANDLE BAR
HOLE SIZE
1¼" (3)
14"
(35.5)
24"
(61)
24"
(61)
HANDLES 2OFF
1¼" OFF CUTS .5"
HANDLE BAR
1¼" HOLE
3" x 1" x 20"
(7.5 x 2.5 x 51)
HOLE FOR 4MM BOLT
20" (51)
WOOD SPACERS 2OFF x 1" THICK.
5"
(13)
HOLE SIZE
1¼" (3)
DRILL FOR 2" RETAINING SCREW.
10" x 2" x 1" 2OFF
HOSE CLIP
WOOD SPACERS 2OFF
5MM PLYBOARD
21½"
(54.5)
1¼" HOLE
7"
(18)
1½" x 1" x 8½" x 8 OFF
(4 x 2.5 x 21.5)
centre pieces of drum

OBELISKS

There are two sizes, one for the larger and one for the smaller garden. They are nearly always painted or stained in various colours such as greens, blues, mauve, black or white. They are made of tiling lathe or batten 1.5" x 1" which is sawn in two lengthways. Use tanalised wood and make sure it is dry; if you buy a small pack, cut the bandings and seperate the wood so that it dries on every side. If you cut some types of wood when they are wet, they feather which makes sandpapering very difficult and painting even harder.

Obelisks are used these days so that plants such as roses, clematis or honeysuckle can climb up through the framework and form a pyramid of scent and colour.

Cut the four long pieces first and then the two longest bottom cross pieces, sandpapering as you go. Mitre saw the top ends and nail up together with the longest cross piece. Don't worry about the cross piece overhangs, they can be sawn off later. Add the rest of the cross pieces, making sure that they are level. For the fixing I use sherardised pins, ring nails or oval nails to avoid splitting the wood.

Mitre cut the top of one of the assemblies, cut the two long 10.5" (26.5cms) cross pieces and fix together. Your obelisk is now beginning to take shape. Add in the rest of the cross pieces and cut off the overhangs, using a tennon saw or jig saw, and then nail up. Although the wood may be tanalised it is best to paint it with a wood preservative; it can then be colour painted if necessary.

SMALL OBELISK

MADE IN 1" x 1" (2.5 x 2.5) BATTEN

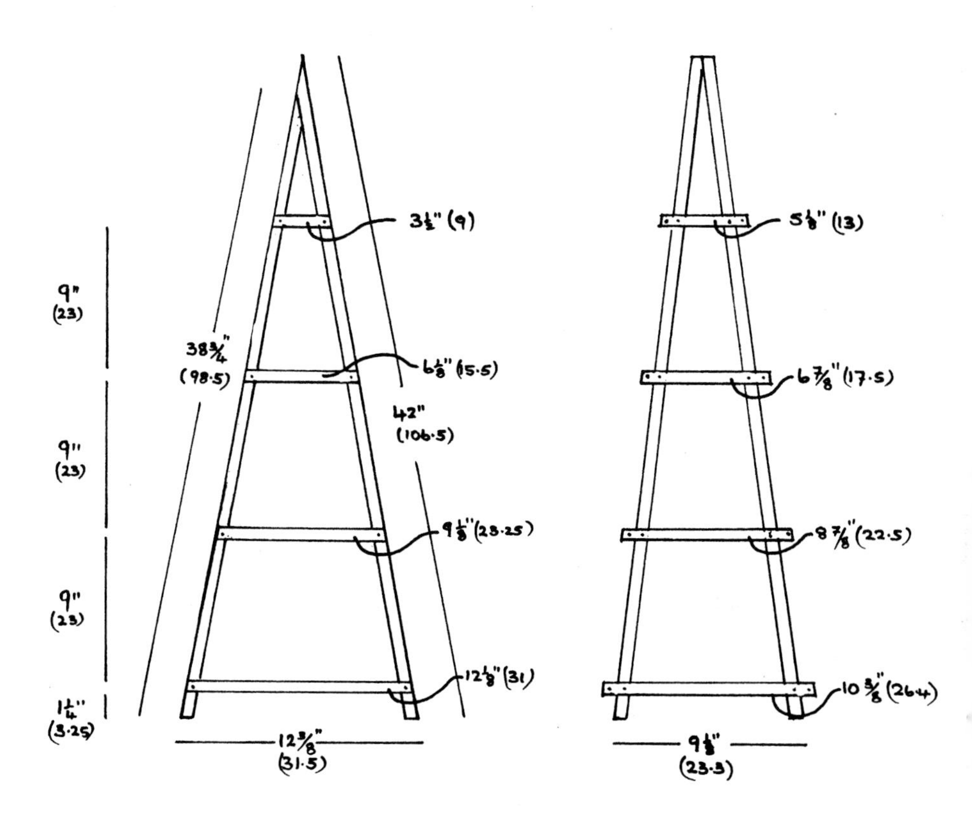

LARGE OBELISK

MADE IN 1" X 1" (2.5 X 2.5) BATTEN

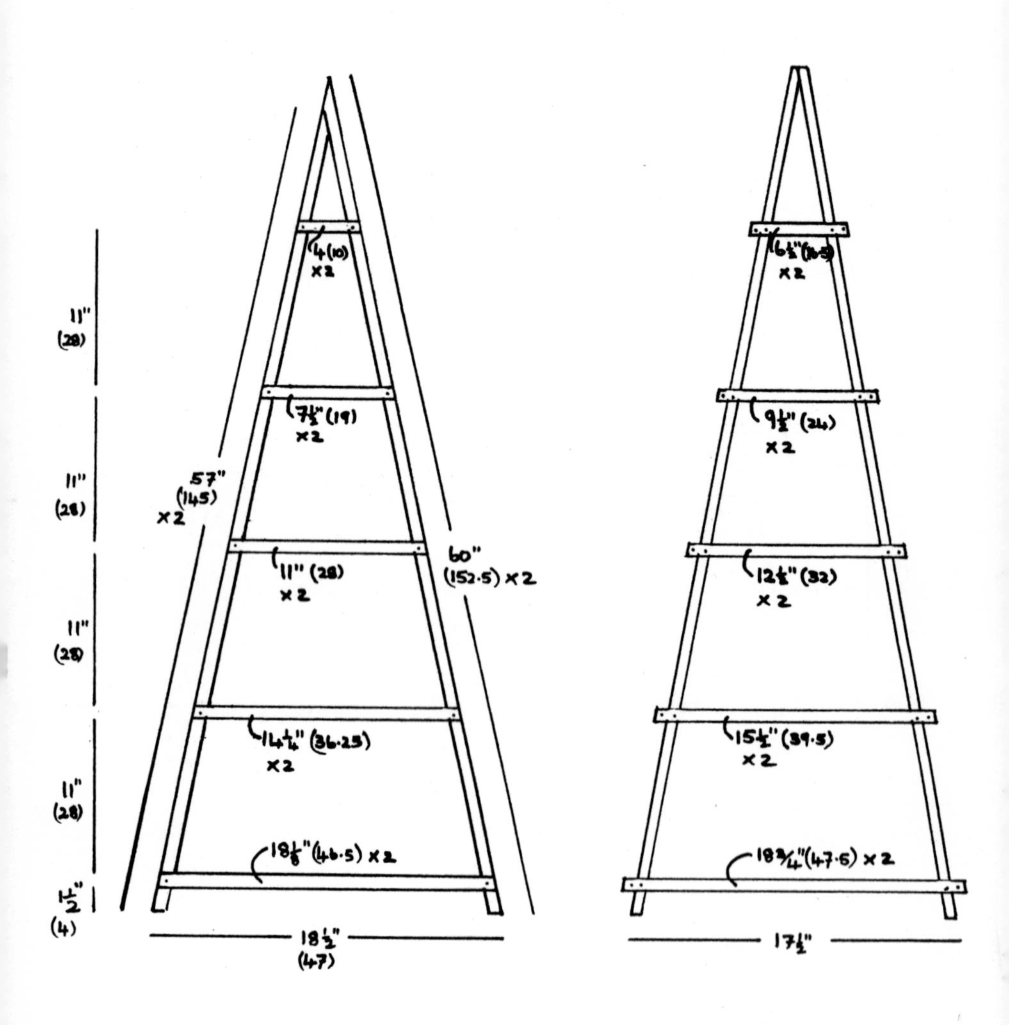

G000293620

2015

JANUARY

M	T	W	T	F	S	S
			01	02	03	04
05	06	07	08	09	10	11
12	13	14	15	16	17	18
19	20	21	22	23	24	25
26	27	28	29	30	31	

FEBRUARY

M	T	W	T	F	S	S
						01
02	03	04	05	06	07	08
09	10	11	12	13	14	15
16	17	18	19	20	21	22
23	24	25	26	27	28	

MARCH

M	T	W	T	F	S	S
						01
02	03	04	05	06	07	08
09	10	11	12	13	14	15
16	17	18	19	20	21	22
23	24	25	26	27	28	29
30	31					

APRIL

M	T	W	T	F	S	S
		01	02	03	04	05
06	07	08	09	10	11	12
13	14	15	16	17	18	19
20	21	22	23	24	25	26
27	28	29	30			

MAY

M	T	W	T	F	S	S
				01	02	03
04	05	06	07	08	09	10
11	12	13	14	15	16	17
18	19	20	21	22	23	24
25	26	27	28	29	30	31

JUNE

M	T	W	T	F	S	S
01	02	03	04	05	06	07
08	09	10	11	12	13	14
15	16	17	18	19	20	21
22	23	24	25	26	27	28
29	30					

JULY

M	T	W	T	F	S	S
		01	02	03	04	05
06	07	08	09	10	11	12
13	14	15	16	17	18	19
20	21	22	23	24	25	26
27	28	29	30	31		

AUGUST

M	T	W	T	F	S	S
					01	02
03	04	05	06	07	08	09
10	11	12	13	14	15	16
17	18	19	20	21	22	23
24	25	26	27	28	29	30
31						

SEPTEMBER

M	T	W	T	F	S	S
	01	02	03	04	05	06
07	08	09	10	11	12	13
14	15	16	17	18	19	20
21	22	23	24	25	26	27
28	29	30				

OCTOBER

M	T	W	T	F	S	S
			01	02	03	04
05	06	07	08	09	10	11
12	13	14	15	16	17	18
19	20	21	22	23	24	25
26	27	28	29	30	31	

NOVEMBER

M	T	W	T	F	S	S
						01
02	03	04	05	06	07	08
09	10	11	12	13	14	15
16	17	18	19	20	21	22
23	24	25	26	27	28	29
30						

DECEMBER

M	T	W	T	F	S	S
	01	02	03	04	05	06
07	08	09	10	11	12	13
14	15	16	17	18	19	20
21	22	23	24	25	26	27
28	29	30	31			

PERSONAL INFORMATION

Name

Address

Home Telephone

Mobile

e-mail

Business Address

Work Telephone

Work Fax

Work e-mail

Car Registration

Driving Licence

Insurance Number

Passport Number

Doctor

Doctor Telephone

Blood Group

Allergies

In case of emergency please call

Name

Address

Telephone

2015 ADVANCE PLANNER

JANUARY

FEBRUARY

MARCH

APRIL

MAY

JUNE

2015 ADVANCE PLANNER

JULY

AUGUST

SEPTEMBER

OCTOBER

NOVEMBER

DECEMBER

MONDAY
29

TUESDAY
30

WEDNESDAY
31

THURSDAY
1

New Year's Holiday (UK & Republic of Ireland)

FRIDAY
2

Holiday (Scotland)

SATURDAY
3

SUNDAY
4

MONDAY
5

TUESDAY
6

WEDNESDAY
7

THURSDAY
8

FRIDAY
9

SATURDAY
10

SUNDAY
11

MONDAY
12

TUESDAY
13

WEDNESDAY
14

THURSDAY
15

FRIDAY
16

SATURDAY
17

SUNDAY
18

MONDAY
19

TUESDAY
20

WEDNESDAY
21

THURSDAY
22

FRIDAY
23

SATURDAY
24

SUNDAY
25

MONDAY
26

TUESDAY
27

WEDNESDAY
28

THURSDAY
29

FRIDAY
30

SATURDAY
31

SUNDAY
1

MONDAY
2

TUESDAY
3

WEDNESDAY
4

THURSDAY
5

FRIDAY
6

SATURDAY
7

SUNDAY
8

MONDAY
9

TUESDAY
10

WEDNESDAY
11

THURSDAY
12

FRIDAY
13

SATURDAY
14

St. Valentine's Day

SUNDAY
15

MONDAY
16

TUESDAY
17

WEDNESDAY
18

Ash Wednesday

THURSDAY
19

Chinese New Year

FRIDAY
20

SATURDAY
21

SUNDAY
22

MONDAY
23

TUESDAY
24

WEDNESDAY
25

THURSDAY
26

FRIDAY
27

SATURDAY
28

SUNDAY
1

St. David's Day (Wales)

MONDAY
2

TUESDAY
3

WEDNESDAY
4

THURSDAY
5

FRIDAY
6

SATURDAY
7

SUNDAY
8

MONDAY
9

TUESDAY
10

WEDNESDAY
11

THURSDAY
12

FRIDAY
13

SATURDAY
14

SUNDAY
15

Mothering Sunday (UK)

MONDAY
16

TUESDAY
17

St. Patrick's Day Holiday (Ireland)

WEDNESDAY
18

THURSDAY
19

FRIDAY
20

SATURDAY
21

SUNDAY
22

MARCH 2015

MONDAY
23

TUESDAY
24

WEDNESDAY
25

THURSDAY
26

FRIDAY
27

SATURDAY
28

SUNDAY
29

Daylight Saving Begins

MONDAY
30

TUESDAY
31

WEDNESDAY
1

THURSDAY
2

FRIDAY
3

Good Friday (UK)

SATURDAY
4

SUNDAY
5

Easter Sunday

MONDAY
6

Easter Monday (UK & Republic of Ireland)

TUESDAY
7

WEDNESDAY
8

THURSDAY
9

FRIDAY
10

SATURDAY
11

SUNDAY
12

MONDAY
13

TUESDAY
14

WEDNESDAY
15

THURSDAY
16

FRIDAY
17

SATURDAY
18

SUNDAY
19

MONDAY
20

TUESDAY
21

WEDNESDAY
22

THURSDAY
23

St. George's Day (England)

FRIDAY
24

SATURDAY
25

SUNDAY
26

MONDAY
27

TUESDAY
28

WEDNESDAY
29

THURSDAY
30

FRIDAY
1

SATURDAY
2

SUNDAY
3

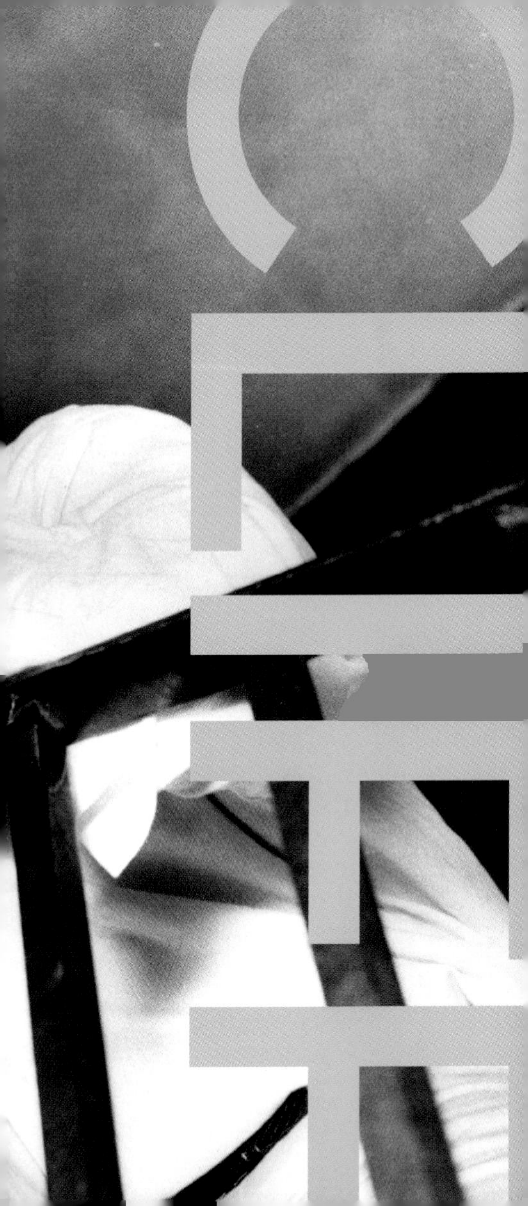

MONDAY
4

May Day Holiday (UK & Republic of Ireland)

TUESDAY
5

WEDNESDAY
6

THURSDAY
7

FRIDAY
8

SATURDAY
9

SUNDAY
10

MONDAY
11

TUESDAY
12

WEDNESDAY
13

THURSDAY
14

FRIDAY
15

SATURDAY
16

SUNDAY
17

MONDAY
18

TUESDAY
19

WEDNESDAY
20

THURSDAY
21

FRIDAY
22

SATURDAY
23

SUNDAY
24

MONDAY
25

Spring Holiday (UK)

TUESDAY
26

WEDNESDAY
27

THURSDAY
28

FRIDAY
29

SATURDAY
30

SUNDAY
31

JUNE 2015

MONDAY
1

TUESDAY
2

WEDNESDAY
3

THURSDAY
4

FRIDAY
5

SATURDAY
6

SUNDAY
7

MONDAY
8

TUESDAY
9

WEDNESDAY
10

THURSDAY
11

FRIDAY
12

SATURDAY
13

SUNDAY
14

MONDAY
15

TUESDAY
16

WEDNESDAY
17

THURSDAY
18

FRIDAY
19

SATURDAY
20

SUNDAY
21

Father's Day / Longest Day

MONDAY
22

TUESDAY
23

WEDNESDAY
24

THURSDAY
25

FRIDAY
26

SATURDAY
27

SUNDAY
28

MONDAY
29

TUESDAY
30

WEDNESDAY
1

THURSDAY
2

FRIDAY
3

SATURDAY
4

SUNDAY
5

MONDAY
6

TUESDAY
7

WEDNESDAY
8

THURSDAY
9

FRIDAY
10

SATURDAY
11

SUNDAY
12

MONDAY
13

Holiday (Northern Ireland)

TUESDAY
14

WEDNESDAY
15

THURSDAY
16

FRIDAY
17

SATURDAY
18

SUNDAY
19

MONDAY
20

TUESDAY
21

WEDNESDAY
22

THURSDAY
23

FRIDAY
24

SATURDAY
25

SUNDAY
26

MONDAY
27

TUESDAY
28

WEDNESDAY
29

THURSDAY
30

FRIDAY
31

SATURDAY
1

SUNDAY
2

MONDAY
3

Holiday (Scotland & Republic of Ireland)

TUESDAY
4

WEDNESDAY
5

THURSDAY
6

FRIDAY
7

SATURDAY
8

SUNDAY
9

AUGUST 2015

MONDAY
10

TUESDAY
11

WEDNESDAY
12

THURSDAY
13

FRIDAY
14

SATURDAY
15

SUNDAY
16

MONDAY
17

TUESDAY
18

WEDNESDAY
19

THURSDAY
20

FRIDAY
21

SATURDAY
22

SUNDAY
23

AUGUST 2015

MONDAY
24

TUESDAY
25

WEDNESDAY
26

THURSDAY
27

FRIDAY
28

SATURDAY
29

SUNDAY
30

MONDAY
31

Late Summer Holiday (UK)

TUESDAY
1

WEDNESDAY
2

THURSDAY
3

FRIDAY
4

SATURDAY
5

SUNDAY
6

SEPTEMBER 2015

MONDAY
7

TUESDAY
8

WEDNESDAY
9

THURSDAY
10

FRIDAY
11

SATURDAY
12

SUNDAY
13

MONDAY
14

Rosh Hashanah (Jewish New Year)

TUESDAY
15

WEDNESDAY
16

THURSDAY
17

FRIDAY
18

SATURDAY
19

SUNDAY
20

MONDAY
21

The United Nations International Day of Peace

TUESDAY
22

WEDNESDAY
23

Yom Kippur (Day of Atonement)

THURSDAY
24

FRIDAY
25

SATURDAY
26

SUNDAY
27

MONDAY
28

TUESDAY
29

WEDNESDAY
30

THURSDAY
1

FRIDAY
2

SATURDAY
3

SUNDAY
4

OCTOBER 2015

MONDAY
5

TUESDAY
6

WEDNESDAY
7

THURSDAY
8

FRIDAY
9

SATURDAY
10

SUNDAY
11

MONDAY
12

TUESDAY
13

WEDNESDAY
14

Al Hijra

THURSDAY
15

FRIDAY
16

SATURDAY
17

SUNDAY
18

OCTOBER 2015

MONDAY
19

TUESDAY
20

WEDNESDAY
21

THURSDAY
22

FRIDAY
23

SATURDAY
24

SUNDAY
25

Daylight Saving Ends

MONDAY
26

Holiday (Republic of Ireland)

TUESDAY
27

WEDNESDAY
28

THURSDAY
29

FRIDAY
30

SATURDAY
31

Halloween

SUNDAY
1

NOVEMBER 2015

MONDAY
2

TUESDAY
3

WEDNESDAY
4

THURSDAY
5

FRIDAY
6

SATURDAY
7

SUNDAY
8

Remembrance Sunday

MONDAY
9

TUESDAY
10

WEDNESDAY
11

Diwali

THURSDAY
12

FRIDAY
13

SATURDAY
14

SUNDAY
15

NOVEMBER 2015

MONDAY
16

TUESDAY
17

WEDNESDAY
18

THURSDAY
19

FRIDAY
20

SATURDAY
21

SUNDAY
22

MONDAY
23

TUESDAY
24

WEDNESDAY
25

THURSDAY
26

FRIDAY
27

SATURDAY
28

SUNDAY
29

MONDAY
30

St. Andrew's Day (Scotland)

TUESDAY
1

WEDNESDAY
2

THURSDAY
3

FRIDAY
4

SATURDAY
5

SUNDAY
6

MONDAY
7

TUESDAY
8

WEDNESDAY
9

THURSDAY
10

FRIDAY
11

SATURDAY
12

SUNDAY
13

DECEMBER 2015

MONDAY
14

TUESDAY
15

WEDNESDAY
16

THURSDAY
17

FRIDAY
18

SATURDAY
19

SUNDAY
20

MONDAY
21

TUESDAY
22

Shortest Day

WEDNESDAY
23

THURSDAY
24

FRIDAY
25

Christmas Day

SATURDAY
26

Boxing Day / St. Stephen's Day (Republic of Ireland)

SUNDAY
27

MONDAY
28

Boxing Day Holiday / St. Stephen's Day Holiday (Republic of Ireland)

TUESDAY
29

WEDNESDAY
30

THURSDAY
31

FRIDAY
1

New Year's Holiday (UK & Republic of Ireland)

SATURDAY
2

SUNDAY
3

2015 NOTABLE DATES

New Year's Holiday (UK & Republic of Ireland)	Jan 1
Holiday (Scotland)	Jan 2
St. Valentine's Day	Feb 14
Ash Wednesday	Feb 18
Chinese New Year	Feb 19
St. David's Day (Wales)	Mar 01
Mothering Sunday (UK)	Mar 15
St. Patrick's Day Holiday (Ireland)	Mar 17
Daylight Saving Begins	Mar 29
Good Friday (UK)	Apr 03
Easter Sunday	Apr 05
Easter Monday (UK & Republic of Ireland)	Apr 06
St. George's Day (England)	Apr 23
May Day Holiday (UK & Republic of Ireland)	May 04
Spring Holiday (UK)	May 25
Father's Day	Jun 21
Longest Day	Jun 21
Holiday (Northern Ireland)	Jul 13
Holiday (Scotland & Republic of Ireland)	Aug 03
Late Summer Holiday (UK)	Aug 31
Rosh Hashanah (Jewish New Year)	Sep 14
The United Nations International Day of Peace	Sep 21
Yom Kippur (Day of Atonement)	Sep 23
Al Hijra	Oct 14
Daylight Saving Ends	Oct 25
Holiday (Republic of Ireland)	Oct 26
Halloween	Oct 31
Remembrance Sunday	Nov 8
Diwali	Nov 11
St. Andrew's Day (Scotland)	Nov 30
Shortest Day	Dec 22
Christmas Day	Dec 25
Boxing Day	Dec 26
St. Stephen's Day (Republic of Ireland)	Dec 26
Boxing Day Holiday	Dec 28
St. Stephen's Day Holiday (Republic of Ireland)	Dec 28

ADDRESS BOOK

Name

Address/Telephone

Name

Address/Telephone

Name

Address/Telephone

Name

Address/Telephone

Name

Address/Telephone

Name

Address/Telephone

Name

Address/Telephone

Name

Address/Telephone

ADDRESS BOOK

Name

Address/Telephone

Name

Address/Telephone

Name

Address/Telephone

Name

Address/Telephone

Name

Address/Telephone

Name

Address/Telephone

Name

Address/Telephone

Name

Address/Telephone

NOTES

2016

JANUARY

M	T	W	T	F	S	S
				01	02	03
04	05	06	07	08	09	10
11	12	13	14	15	16	17
18	19	20	21	22	23	24
25	26	27	28	29	30	31

FEBRUARY

M	T	W	T	F	S	S
01	02	03	04	05	06	07
08	09	10	11	12	13	14
15	16	17	18	19	20	21
22	23	24	25	26	27	28
29						

MARCH

M	T	W	T	F	S	S
	01	02	03	04	05	06
07	08	09	10	11	12	13
14	15	16	17	18	19	20
21	22	23	24	25	26	27
28	29	30	31			

APRIL

M	T	W	T	F	S	S
				01	02	03
04	05	06	07	08	09	10
11	12	13	14	15	16	17
18	19	20	21	22	23	24
25	26	27	28	29	30	

MAY

M	T	W	T	F	S	S
						01
02	03	04	05	06	07	08
09	10	11	12	13	14	15
16	17	18	19	20	21	22
23	24	25	26	27	28	29
30	31					

JUNE

M	T	W	T	F	S	S
		01	02	03	04	05
06	07	08	09	10	11	12
13	14	15	16	17	18	19
20	21	22	23	24	25	26
27	28	29	30			

JULY

M	T	W	T	F	S	S
				01	02	03
04	05	06	07	08	09	10
11	12	13	14	15	16	17
18	19	20	21	22	23	24
25	26	27	28	29	30	31

AUGUST

M	T	W	T	F	S	S
01	02	03	04	05	06	07
08	09	10	11	12	13	14
15	16	17	18	19	20	21
22	23	24	25	26	27	28
29	30	31				

SEPTEMBER

M	T	W	T	F	S	S
			01	02	03	04
05	06	07	08	09	10	11
12	13	14	15	16	17	18
19	20	21	22	23	24	25
26	27	28	29	30		

OCTOBER

M	T	W	T	F	S	S
					01	02
03	04	05	06	07	08	09
10	11	12	13	14	15	16
17	18	19	20	21	22	23
24	25	26	27	28	29	30
31						

NOVEMBER

M	T	W	T	F	S	S
	01	02	03	04	05	06
07	08	09	10	11	12	13
14	15	16	17	18	19	20
21	22	23	24	25	26	27
28	29	30				

DECEMBER

M	T	W	T	F	S	S
			01	02	03	04
05	06	07	08	09	10	11
12	13	14	15	16	17	18
19	20	21	22	23	24	25
26	27	28	29	30	31	

Published and Printed by Danilo Promotions Limited, Unit 3,
The io Centre, Lea Road, Waltham Abbey, EN9 1AS. Printed in South Korea.